This is a beautiful book, full of consoling and helpful approaches to our spiritual life. This is also a serious book, one written with a view to eternity and asking us on every page to be honest about where we are and where we're headed. Above all, though, these pages carry the honest and sincere confession of a truly priestly heart, a heart which burns with one desire: that you be saved and, indeed, "that all men be saved." I hope that like mine, your experience of this book will be a healing, sobering, and liberating immersion into the sacred fire of Christ's love.

Timothy Patitsas
Author, *The Ethics of Beauty*

Toolkit for Spiritual Growth II by Fr. Evan Armatas is an essential guide to inform Orthodox Christians and spiritual seekers how to develop more spiritual disciplines and to see time in a richer way. In Fr. Evan's usual thoughtful and pastoral approach, he guides us to the deep wells of Orthodox praxis, providing timeless wisdom and practical steps so that we can unite every aspect of our lives to Christ. This welcomed work is a must-read for those who desire to "draw near to God" (James 4:8).

Fr. Tom Soroka
Host of *Ancient Faith Today Live with Fr. Tom Soroka*

Readers will benefit from Fr. Evan's years of pastoral experience, wisdom, and love. In this book, he offers himself to each person who comes to him and, as he shares about the Scriptures, confession, and time as spiritual tools, he communicates something deeper, or rather someone greater: Christ Himself, who cannot be captured in dogmas, debates, and descriptions. This work is not simply an introduction to spiritual tools but an invitation and encouragement to draw closer to Christ and encounter the fullness of life that can only be found in the embrace of God.

Dr. Philip Mamalakis
Associate Professor Pastoral Care
Holy Cross Greek Orthodox School of Theology

We are thrilled to endorse the second volume of *Toolkit for Spiritual Growth*. Building on the foundation of his first book, Fr. Evan continues to masterfully present powerful, time-tested spiritual tools that help the faithful live out the Orthodox Faith in their daily lives. His insights not only deepen our understanding of the Church's rich Tradition but also empower us to apply it in meaningful, transformative ways. We are confident that this book will serve as a treasured resource for readers for years to come.

Rev. Dr. Nicholas and Dr. Roxanne Louh
Hosts of *Live with the Louhs* podcast
Authors of *Renewing You* and *6 Hours, 7 Lessons*

Father Evan Armatas immediately brings you into the story in *Toolkit for Spiritual Growth II* through his warm, inviting, familial writing style. He succinctly and informatively adds three more tools to our spiritual toolbelts. With every page and every footnote, I got more excited to learn how each of these disciplines can help me in my life journey as a son, husband, parent, colleague, and leader. Thank you, Fr. Evan!

Constantine M. Triantafilou
Executive Director and CEO,
International Orthodox Christian Charities

Do you ever wish for more clarity and direction? Do you ever find yourself craving more peace, perspective, and transformative moments? If so, this book is for you! With humility, relatability, and deep wisdom, Fr. Evan helps us understand the Master Carpenter so that we can live and love like Him. These tools are for everyone, at any point in your faith journey, and learning to apply them will free you from worldly distractions and anchor you to eternal truth.

Kari Kampakis
Bestselling author of *Love Her Well*
and host of the *Girl Mom* podcast

In his first volume of *Toolkit for Spiritual Growth*, Fr. Evan Armatas showed us the three-legged stool on which our spiritual advancement is anchored—prayer, fasting, and almsgiving. Now in Volume Two, he goes further in showing us the importance of Scripture reading, confession, and living in the present moment of time. These are not abstract concepts but rather practical, day-to-day tools we can actually use on our spiritual journey. I'm grateful for the profound simplicity of these words.

John Maddex
Retired Founder and CEO
Ancient Faith Ministries

Father Evan once again, through his unique and personable conversational and story-telling style, offers his readers practical wisdom to be implemented in their spiritual life. Covering subjects as vast as Holy Scripture, the Sacrament of Confession, and the "simple" concept of time, Fr. Evan presents them in a way that is understandable to all and applicable by all.

Fr. George Dokos, ThD
Holy Apostles Orthodox Church, Westchester, IL
Author of *Made for Union: The Sacramental Spirituality of St. Nikodemos of the Holy Mountain*

Father Evan has distilled the Church's theology to the essentials without compromising her profound depth. With great love and care, he illuminates sacred truths we didn't even realize we needed, such as his insights on the theology of time. This book speaks to people at all stages of the spiritual life. I am deeply grateful to Fr. Evan and his ministry, which continues to draw me closer to Christ.

Alexis Pappas
Director, Effective Christian Ministry Cohort
Department of Youth and Young Adult Ministries
Greek Orthodox Archdiocese of America

Just as you cannot build a house without the proper tools, so too you cannot live an overcoming life (John 16:33) without practical guidance. Both of Fr. Evan's *Toolkit for Spiritual Growth* books serve as practical partners in your journey from glory to glory.

Hank Hanegraaff
President, Christian Research Institute
Author, Host of *The Bible Answer Man* and *Hank Unplugged*

TOOLKIT *for*
SPIRITUAL GROWTH II

*A Practical Guide
to Scripture, Confession, and Time*

Fr. Evan Armatas

ANCIENT FAITH PUBLISHING
CHESTERTON, INDIANA

Toolkit for Spiritual Growth II: A Practical Guide to Scripture, Confession, and Time
Copyright © 2025 Evan Armatas

Published by:
Ancient Faith Publishing
A Division of Ancient Faith Ministries
1050 Broadway, Suite 6
Chesterton, IN 46304

Unless otherwise noted, Scripture quotations are taken from the New King James Version, © 1979, 1980, 1982 by Thomas Nelson, Inc. Used by permission.

Cover art and design: Ephrosini Candelario

ISBN: 978-1-955890-81-6

Library of Congress Control Number: 2025938700

To my wife and best friend, Stacy;
to my lovely daughters, Alexia, Eleni, and Maria;
and to my beloved son, Spyridon.
I love walking through this life with you.

Contents

Foreword

IT IS WITH MUCH JOY and anticipation for the devoted that I recommend *Toolkit for Spiritual Growth II* by Fr. Evan Armatas. This book, his second about the spiritual tools of the Church, offers readers the opportunity to come closer to our Lord in a manner that is practical. This book is not just to be read, but to be applied with prayer.

Father Evan has taken the time to convey a strong and meaningful message that involves each of us as faithful Orthodox Christians. The words allow readers to have a deeper understanding about the importance of Scripture reading, participating in the Holy Sacrament of Confession and comprehending why we confess, and living in the present moment. I encourage you to read through this book with prayer, and I embolden you to find a spiritual father to help guide you through this sacred journey of transformation in Christ.

Father Evan's work in the parish of Saint Spyridon in Loveland, Colorado, is legendary, and through his efforts, and the work of the Holy Spirit, many have been brought to Christ. Conveying my congratulations to him for this book, I thank him for his many contributions in reclaiming the Great Commission (Matt. 28:18–20).

+CONSTANTINE
Metropolitan of Denver
Greek Orthodox Archdiocese of America

Preface

ONLY A FEW MONTHS INTO serving as a parish priest I was asked to lead a retreat for teenagers. The topic I chose for the retreat was "The Spiritual Tools of the Church." Now, I am fond of using object lessons, and so I devised one for my opening talk. I collected a bunch of tools—a hammer, screwdrivers (Phillips head and standard), a wrench, a tape measure, and other supplies. I also got a tool belt and some nails, wood, screws, and other construction items.

My talk began with a simple analogy. I told the teens that in the Church we have various spiritual tools, or disciplines. These tools, I went on to explain, help us build a spiritual life. Moreover, master builders have learned which tools can be used and how they can assist us in erecting a life that is true and beautiful. These builders, often called saints, have shared techniques and hard-earned skills that were revealed to them by the Master Builder, Jesus Christ (Matt. 7:24–27; 1 Cor. 3:9–15). They have used these tools within the Lord's great workshop, His Church.

I laid out all the tools, and we talked about how each one is used in construction. A hammer is used to hit things, but carpenters don't just bang on wood. Rather, they know how to use the hammer skillfully. Nor do they use a hammer on a screw or use a tape measure to apply an adhesive. Moreover, carpenters often wear a tool belt and place the tools in it so that without looking they can grab just the one they need.

I then asked for volunteers and blindfolded them. Next, I gave them a series of challenges related to various construction tasks. They quickly realized how important it is to know the tools, where they are, and how they are used when attempting to build.

In my first book, *Toolkit for Spiritual Growth: A Practical Guide to Prayer, Fasting, and Almsgiving*, I discussed three of the primary tools that Christ shared with His followers. These tools, I said, "free us from the disordered way of life that has become normal for many, even though their hearts and minds tell them otherwise. These spiritual practices put us back together in a rightly ordered way and lead us into life."[1]

Not long after sharing these tools, I heard from readers who wanted to know what other tools might be helpful. Honestly, there are dozens, and picking which ones to share next was not easy. In this sequel, I have taken up three more spiritual tools: Scripture, confession, and time. The pattern of this book is similar to that of the first. I share a mixture of theology and practical advice, weaving in stories that help illustrate my points. I have drawn on the wisdom of Scripture and the life of the Church: her services, hymns, traditions, and rhythms; the teachings of the saints and Fathers; and years of pastoral experience. In some ways, I am trying to share with readers the experience of sitting down one on one with me.

I think these three disciplines, along with those from the first book, will provide additional support to anyone who seeks to live a transfigured life in Christ—a life centered in truth and focused on

---

1   Fr. Evan Armatas, *Toolkit for Spiritual Growth: A Practical Guide to Prayer, Fasting, and Almsgiving* (Ancient Faith Publishing, 2020), 7.

beauty. Our goal is holiness and the Kingdom of God. I hope you will find that the spiritual tools the Lord revealed to us are timeless and perfectly suited to heal us and make us truly human. For all of us who wonder if this is truly possible, I share the invitation given by the Lord during His ministry on earth: "Come and see" (John 1:39).

CHAPTER ONE

How to Read Scripture

EOPLE WHO COME TO SAINT Spyridon are often experiencing Orthodox Christianity for the first time during the Divine Liturgy. Yet, the Liturgy wasn't designed to be the first stop someone makes on their way into a relationship with Christ and His Body, the Church. This means that without any reference or basis for what is happening, a guest's experience of the service and of Christianity is like watching a foreign film without subtitles, which means it often doesn't make sense—at least not on the surface.[2]

I have made a practice of keeping an eye out for these new people. After their initial visit, I send them a personal invitation to speak with me about their thoughts and questions. I want to make sure they get some time with me and other people in the community right from the start. This serves a twofold purpose: First, it

---

2   In the ancient past, inquirers into the Christian Faith stayed in the Divine Liturgy only through the reading of the Holy Scriptures. This part of the Liturgy came to be called the Liturgy of the Catechumens. There is some wisdom in this ancient practice. The Church recognized that "subtitles" were needed in order to comprehend better the mystery of the Faith. What is important to our discussion here is the fact that the Scriptures formed this subtext.

gives them an opportunity to have their questions answered, and second, it helps them begin forming relationships and connecting with the community.[3]

I also know firsthand that a journey into the Gospels and the Christian way of life is a lot to take in and assimilate. Any one of us, whether we grew up in the Church or have just begun our investigation into the life of Christ, can be misled or confused, especially when our journey is not rooted in the truth and beauty of the Scriptures as rightly interpreted in the Church. This is why it is also a practice of mine to reach out consistently to established members of the community as well. They too need time with their priest to explore the questions they have and to be instructed in the Faith. For over twenty years I have offered a weekly Bible study, and the teachings of Scripture as understood by Christ's Body, the Church, form the basis for every teaching offered in our community.[4]

In my many years of meeting with people, I could share countless stories that illustrate the primacy of the Bible in the life of the Church—stories that demonstrate the importance of the Holy Scriptures and their connection to the life of the community. However, one story stands out, and it just so happens that it involves someone who was brand new to Christianity.

---

3   Onboarding new people into the Christian Faith is an essential task of the local Christian community/parish and its leaders. Creating a culture of welcome and belonging is an important prerequisite in this process. This culture is not developed by just one or two people in the parish but is the responsibility of every Christian. This spirit of hospitality is rooted in an understanding of God's love and is a response to it.

4   If you are interested in downloading the Bible study I offer, you can find me on most platforms and specifically at Ancient Faith Ministries (ancientfaith.com) and at my parish's website (saintspyridon.church). The Bible study is called "Transforming Our Lives in Christ."

Chelsea

A FEW YEARS AGO I met Chelsea, a clinical psychologist, after Liturgy one Sunday. She was accompanying her husband, who was investigating a return to Christianity.[5] Only a few months earlier they had moved to Fort Collins, Colorado, the town just north of my parish, and they had started visiting various Christian churches.

After spending several months doing what some call "church shopping," they had reached a point of giving up. They were dissatisfied with what they were experiencing. Thus far, nothing struck them as particularly deep, and their visits to churches had been unconvincing, especially for Chelsea.[6] Her husband proposed what he thought was "something unfamiliar and unknown by many"—the Orthodox Church. He explained to her that from what he had read, this "other church" might just be different from all the churches they had visited so far.

Before attending, Chelsea's husband sent me an email asking if they could come.[7] Of course, I said yes, and they attended a few

---

5   This is not an unusual occurrence today. Many people who grew up Christian have left the Faith for one reason or another. It has been my experience that their departure is often rooted in a set of misunderstandings about Christ and/or what the Christian Faith teaches on a whole set of ideas such as sin, salvation, faith, the Church, and the sacraments.

6   Chelsea and her husband's experience is not unusual. To make matters worse, many tell me that when visiting a church, they often go unnoticed and unwelcomed. I am saddened to hear that even seekers who attend an Orthodox parish after searching long and hard for truth and beauty end up sitting alone for weeks, never being greeted or made to feel welcomed. It is essential that people who come to church, whether they are new or returning members, feel a deep sense of welcome and belonging. I would add that engaging people in the life of the parish in a meaningful way is one additional element that cannot be overlooked. I've begun using the acronym WEB, to think about how we should treat people who come to church: We should *welcome* them and *engage* them so they may feel they *belong*.

7   See my previous book *Reclaiming the Great Commission: A Roadmap to Parish Health* (Ancient Faith, 2022) for a look at why many people today

---

times before I had an opportunity to meet with them. After a few meetings, I explained that it would be good to meet with each of them separately. I wanted them to have an opportunity to build a relationship with me and time to ask questions that were specific to their own journey.[8] This was especially important for Chelsea, since this exploration was not initially her idea.

Building a relationship with one's priest and other members of the community is an essential part of becoming a Christian. For some today, the ideas of community, of the Church, and of spiritual leadership have been lost. However, there is not one saint in the Christian Faith who followed a path devoid of community, and there is no wisdom or truth in going at it alone.

Rather, life in Christ has always been connected to the Church. It has always been communal, just as all that God does is Trinitarian.[9] This is especially true when it comes to understanding the Scriptures. We don't interpret or read them on our own. Saint Peter explained this when he wrote, "[Know] this first, that no prophecy of Scripture is of any private interpretation, for prophecy never came by the will of man, but holy men of God spoke *as they were* moved by the Holy Spirit" (2 Pet. 1:20–21). Notice that St. Peter directs Christians toward a communal understanding of the Scriptures and away from any individual interpretation. This is an essential point.

Chelsea arrived at the church one morning for her appointment with me. My office is set up casually on purpose. It isn't filled with shelves of books; rather, there is a round coffee table, icons, artwork,

---

would feel the need to ask whether or not it is okay to attend an Orthodox service—and why that is a big problem.

8   An important element in our Christian walk is spiritual guidance and mentorship. This is especially true when it comes to the Holy Scriptures.

9   We may not often consider that every act of Christ involved the Father and the Holy Spirit. There is never a moment in which the Persons of the Trinity are alone and separate (John 10:30).

lots of light, plants, and snacks. I want the space to convey a spirit of welcome and hospitality. I think this is more conducive to open conversation and dialogue.

After offering Chelsea some refreshments, I said, "I bet you never thought you'd be sitting in the office of an Orthodox priest!"

Chelsea laughed and said, "That's right. I could never have imagined this." She went on to say that although she never envisioned herself considering Christianity, she had to admit that her experiences thus far in the Orthodox Church had gotten her wondering about things. She had noticed that there was something beautiful and mysterious going on in the Liturgy and with the people she had met so far. The difficulty was that she was unable to articulate exactly what it was that had caught her attention and moved her so deeply.

Starting with the basics, I said, "Tell me, Chelsea, what do you know about Christianity?"

She replied, "Not much."

I find that many who come to Saint Spyridon know very little about Christianity. In this way Chelsea was not alone. Sometimes all that our guests know about the Christian Faith are the cultural icons of Santa Claus and the Easter Bunny, but not much else.

She didn't have an accurate or full picture of who Jesus is, what He teaches, and how that might transform our lives. She had never read the Bible or attended church regularly. Her knowledge was very limited. I think at best she thought of Christianity as a religion with a particular and antiquated set of rules and requirements.

After she shared this, I wondered how I might be able to help her, so I asked, "How do you think I can best assist you?"[10]

---

10 Although the way to salvation comes only through Jesus Christ (John 14:6), each person is different. They need direct pastoral care. I am surprised to learn how unique this approach can be to those who encounter it. They either have not experienced this before within the Christian circles they have walked in or did not know such personal pastoral care existed.

Her response went something like this: "I am not sure. I mean, where do you think I should start?"

Right off the bat, I knew it was a genuine question. She wasn't trying for a "gotcha" of some sort, so I took her question seriously. I stopped and said a prayer silently in my heart for help: "God, what do I share with her? How do I get her started?"

The answer that seemed clear to me was to have her read from the Holy Scriptures, specifically 1 Corinthians 13. This particular passage by St. Paul is well known to most Christians, and this familiarity can cause a Christian to become calloused and lose sight of just how unique and powerful St. Paul's words are. On the other hand, for someone who has never read what he wrote, encountering the passage can be life changing.

After praying, I told Chelsea that I'd like her to read a section of the Bible with me.

"Sure," she said, "but you will have to show me where and what to read."

"No problem," I said, and I opened the Bible to 1 Corinthians and placed the thirteenth chapter in front of her. She began to read the words, "Though I speak with the tongues of men and of angels, but have not love, I have become sounding brass or a clanging cymbal." As Chelsea continued reading, she began to gently weep. The experience of her tears touched me, and I too was moved. I had become desensitized to this passage because I had read it so many times; I had begun to take St. Paul's words for granted.[11] Now

---

11   Anyone who has read the Bible will find it hard to find familiar passages engaging. The truth is that familiar verses can be overlooked, and we can feel as if the meanings of a particular passage have been mined already. This is rarely the case, and even passages we have read hundreds of times have something to offer us. This experience of new insight has happened to me countless times, as it has for others. Just when I think there is nothing

I was hearing the passage anew through her reading of it, and I saw again the truth and beauty conveyed in the words of Holy Scripture. Here is the entire chapter. I'd suggest that you read this slowly and attentively:

> Though I speak with the tongues of men and of angels, but have not love, I have become sounding brass or a clanging cymbal. And though I have *the gift of* prophecy, and understand all mysteries and all knowledge, and though I have all faith, so that I could remove mountains, but have not love, I am nothing. And though I bestow all my goods to feed *the poor*, and though I give my body to be burned, but have not love, it profits me nothing.
>
> Love suffers long *and* is kind; love does not envy; love does not parade itself, is not puffed up; does not behave rudely, does not seek its own, is not provoked, thinks no evil; does not rejoice in iniquity, but rejoices in the truth; bears all things, believes all things, hopes all things, endures all things.
>
> Love never fails. But whether *there are* prophecies, they will fail; whether *there are* tongues, they will cease; whether *there is* knowledge, it will vanish away. For we know in part and we prophesy in part. But when that which is perfect has come, then that which is in part will be done away.
>
> When I was a child, I spoke as a child, I understood as a child, I thought as a child; but when I became a man, I put away childish things. For now we see in a mirror, dimly, but then face to face. Now I know in part, but then I shall know just as I also am known.
>
> And now abide faith, hope, love, these three; but the greatest of these *is* love. (1 Corinthians 13)

---

more to be gleaned from the Bible, I am surprised to discover another truth that changes me for the better.

When Chelsea finished reading the passage, I asked her what had brought tears to her eyes. Her response was not unexpected: "Father Evan, I have always hoped that something like this could be true." Despite her impressive education and experience with the human condition, she had come to realize deep within that something was decidedly missing from her life—something that transcended what she knew. The deepest part of herself had been longing to hear the truth articulated, and this truth is found in the Bible.

What happened next totally threw me. As I was processing what she said, she began sobbing. She seemed overcome with sorrow, and as she wept again, I felt powerless. All I could do was sit with her as her shoulders shook and her tears flowed. When I felt that it was okay to talk, I said, "Chelsea, tell me, what's happening in your heart?"

After a pause, she said something I will never forget: "Father, now that I know this is true, what if I don't find what he is writing about here at Saint Spyridon? Where would I go?"

I was floored. She recognized the truth but was immediately scared at the possibility that it might not be *here*, here in the Church, here in this community. Her experience is similar to falling in love with someone only to find they don't feel the same. It's painful to be around something like that, to realize that your deepest longing is not attainable.

I think it is important to understand that Holy Scripture was the starting point for Chelsea's realizations. It articulated for Chelsea, as it has for countless others, the truth and beauty of God's revelation. Moreover, it also articulated for Chelsea a connected reality: She needed to find this truth and beauty in the parish, in the Church. The Bible and the community are connected. Somehow she realized, without my saying a thing about it, that these words of St. Paul had to be embodied and lived in the local community. The community had to be a witness and perhaps a guide to what she had just read. She needed a connection to exist between the Bible and the people of God, and she knew that if it didn't, she'd be lost.

The same holds true for each of us. This is an important point we need to accept: There is no Bible without the Church. Historically speaking, we know this to be true. It was the Church that assembled the New Testament. It was the Church, the living community of Christ, that laid down not only what books are contained in the Bible but how these books are understood.

Chelsea's story, like many others, is not finished with their first reading of the Bible. Rather, it continues in the communities they join.

Love, Community, and the Bible

IN ONE OF THE LAST exams I took in seminary, I learned an important lesson. Like my classmates, I had come to the end of a series of required classes that were listed in the course catalog in sequence: Dogmatics I, Dogmatics II, and Dogmatics III. Each of these one-year classes was taught by Fr. Emmanuel, a scholar of systematic theology. The subject matter was at times demanding. It was in this series of classes that we studied and discussed the theology of the Church.[12] At the end of three intense years, we approached our final exam. Father Emmanuel explained that our last test would be a class discussion of the question "What will make you a successful priest?"

On our last day my classmates and I came with copious notes from the past three years, and in an attempt to answer his question, we debated points of theology. The result was a cacophony of ideas and a theological stalemate; no one seemed to have the right

---

12   There should be some discomfort when saying we study theology. Studying God and His revelations is never the point. Rather, we must know and live these truths.

answer. At the conclusion of this impassioned exchange of views, Fr. Emmanuel spoke up and asked if we wanted to know the answer. "Yes," we cried while each of us took out a fresh sheet of paper.

Here is his answer: "Inasmuch as you create communities of love, you will be successful as parish priests."

That was it.

After three years of study and hundreds of reading assignments, the answer was love—just as Chelsea had discovered.

Over the past twenty years I have thought a lot about what Fr. Emmanuel said. He was right. Holy Scripture is meant to lead us into love—love of God and love of neighbor. Jesus put it this way: "'You shall love the Lord your God with all your heart, with all your soul, and with all your mind.' This is the first and great commandment. And *the* second *is* like it: 'You shall love your neighbor as yourself.' On these two commandments hang all the Law and the Prophets" (Matt. 22:37b–40). The commandments to love are clear and should continue to guide our communities. Saint Paul taught the same to the churches he fostered, and this is why he exhorted them with the words, "Watch, stand fast in the faith, be brave, be strong. Let all *that* you *do* be done with love" (1 Cor. 16:13–14).

This love was something Chelsea had longed for and then found at Saint Spyridon. She recognized that the Bible teaches us to love, and the community needs to reflect this central truth. It is Holy Scripture that not only defines what is healthy—a loving community—but provides the way to establish it. It guides us by shaping the interactions we have within the church and with those outside it. Jesus taught as much when He said, "A new commandment I give to you, that you love one another; as I have loved you, that you also love one another. By this all will know that you are My disciples, if you have love for one another" (John 13:34–35).

Without question, building the type of community that Christ commanded us to build is not easy. It is also true that whatever we establish will be imperfect and changing. It is only in heaven that we will fully experience what Christ revealed to us. Yet, this truth should not keep us from doing everything we can to create local parishes that emulate the teachings of Christ. Each of us is responsible for the creation of a community in which people like Chelsea will find what they have read about in the Holy Scriptures.

One of my favorite photos is of Chelsea coming out of the baptismal font. From time to time when my own faith wavers, I look again at this photo. Chelsea and her husband, along with their son, are members of our parish. When I finished writing this section I wanted to go over it with her, and once again the two of us were transported to that day in my office. Thankfully, Chelsea and others have found that the truths of the Bible are lived out in our local parish. As she would say, she can't believe how gracious God has been to her and how her life has been transformed.

Scripture and the Church

WHEN I FIRST ARRIVED AT seminary, I met a priest named Fr. Cleopas. He was the registrar at Holy Cross. In our first meeting, I remember asking him—and this is embarrassing to admit—where his name came from. With an incredulous look on his face, he answered me, "From the Bible." I came to learn that Cleopas was one of two men who met Jesus after His Resurrection, on a road that led to a village named Emmaus (Luke 24:18). Over the course of the next few years, I would repeatedly demonstrate my scriptural ignorance. Time and again I'd ask a question only to find that the answer was the same: "It is from the Bible." Whether it was someone's name, a so-called tradition, or even the phrasing found in a hymn, I came to understand that what we do in the Church finds its basis in Holy Scripture.

One example of this is the tradition of parishioners offering a decorated platter of boiled wheat on behalf of a loved one who has passed away. This dish of boiled wheat, mixed with sweet spices, was called "sea-ta-ree" by my grandmother, my *yiayia*.[13] For centuries Christians, when commemorating a loved one, have placed boiled wheat in the church in front of Christ on the icon screen.[14]

As a child I never questioned why this was done, nor did I understand the purpose. Later I came to find out that *sea-ta-ree* is the pronunciation of the Greek word σιτάρι (*sitári*), which means "wheat." Yet I still didn't understand why someone would bring this dish to church when remembering their loved ones. The answer, as you might guess, is found in the Bible. In the Gospel of John, we read the following words of Jesus:

> The hour has come that the Son of Man should be glorified. Most assuredly, I say to you, unless a grain of wheat falls into the ground and dies, it remains alone; but if it dies, it produces much grain. He who loves his life will lose it, and he who hates his life in this world will keep it for eternal life. (John 12:23–25)

In this passage Jesus is speaking about His coming death and Resurrection. To help people understand what is about to happen,

---

13 This dish, also called *kollyva*, contains honey or sugar, pomegranate seeds, and almonds, among other things. The pomegranate is an ancient symbol of eternal life. The almonds are connected in Numbers 17 to the establishment of the priesthood that is later fulfilled in Christ and is also connected to Christ's sacrifice and Resurrection.

14 When the main service of the Divine Liturgy reaches its conclusion, the priest comes out from behind the icon screen to stand before the kollyva and offer the memorial service on behalf of the deceased. Afterward, the family shares this dish with the community.

He uses the example of a grain of wheat being placed in the ground. This is a reference to His sacrifice on the Cross, His death, and burial in a tomb. The Lord is comparing what is about to happen to the burying of a wheat kernel during a season of planting. It too seemingly dies, and from that "death" it brings forth a harvest. It brings forth new life—a harvest not of one kernel but thousands. This natural cycle of planting is in a way miraculous, and Jesus is connecting our eventual death and the decision to follow Him to new life and our entrance into eternity. It is with this in mind that the practice of offering boiled wheat was instituted. One could say that in the offering of this dish Christians are reminded of the words of Christ and our central hope: that Jesus Christ's death on the Cross opens the Kingdom of God to all who follow Him.

Sunday Worship and the Eucharist

ON PURPOSE, I CHOSE THIS example of the boiled wheat to make a point. Even the small things we do in Church are connected to the Bible in a profound way. Of course, this holds true for the larger and more important teachings and actions of the Church. For example, on Sundays, Orthodox Christians celebrate the Divine Liturgy. During the Liturgy we receive the risen Body and Blood of our Lord and Savior Jesus Christ. This singular focus and celebration of Christ's victory over death, and our participation in it through the partaking of Holy Communion every Sunday, has not changed since the time of the apostles. However, over the years, visitors and many Christians have asked me why we haven't "evolved" or changed our service. They wonder why we persist in doing the *same thing* every Sunday. The answer is that this is what we find in the Bible. Let me explain.

Returning to the Gospel of Luke and the story of Cleopas, we find the answer to our question of why Orthodox Christians celebrate the Divine Liturgy and receive the Eucharist *every* Sunday.[15] The passage begins by telling us that on the first day of the week (Luke 24:1), which is Sunday, some women went to the place where Jesus had been buried in order to anoint His body. When they arrived, they found the Tomb empty and were told by two "men"—we understand these men to be angels—"Why do you seek the living among the dead? He is not here, but is risen!" (Luke 24:4, 24:5b–6a). After they returned to the place where the disciples and others who followed the Lord were gathered, Peter, the leader of the disciples, ran to the Tomb and found it empty, just as the women had proclaimed.

Later that day Cleopas and his travel companion, Luke (Luke 24:13), who had witnessed that day's events, left Jerusalem and made their way on foot to a village called Emmaus. While they walked, they were discussing the news that they had just received and the recent events surrounding Jesus' betrayal, arrest, and Crucifixion. At this point in their journey, the resurrected Lord Jesus Christ joins them. However, they do not realize it is Jesus. He begins a dialogue, noticing that their conversation is tinged with sadness and regret (Luke 24:17). In time they share the reason for their disappointments:

> We were hoping that it was He [Jesus] who was going to redeem Israel. Indeed, besides all this, today is the third day since these things happened. Yes, and certain women of our company, who arrived at the tomb early, astonished us. When they did not find His body, they came saying that they had also seen a vision of angels who said He was alive. (Luke 24:21–23)

---

15 Sunday is the first and central day of Christian worship and has remained so since the Resurrection of Christ. The word *Eucharist* comes from Luke 22:19 (εὐχαριστήσας). It is a Greek word meaning "to give thanks." We also refer to this holy mystery (sacrament) as Holy Communion.

They even tell Jesus that some of the disciples and other follow-ers had gone to the Tomb to check and see if what the women had shared was true. In response to their confusion and disbelief, Jesus says to them, "'O foolish ones, and slow of heart to believe in all that the prophets have spoken! Ought not the Christ to have suf-fered these things and to enter into His glory?' And beginning at Moses and all the Prophets, He expounded to them in all the Scrip-tures the things concerning Himself" (Luke 24:25–27).

Oddly enough, this explanation does not lead to the men rec-ognizing that their teacher is the Teacher, Jesus. Instead, as they get close to the village of Emmaus, the two urge Jesus to stay with them. This is what happens next: "Now it came to pass, as He sat at the table with them, that He took bread, blessed and broke *it*, and gave it to them.[16] Then their eyes were opened and they knew Him; and He vanished from their sight" (Luke 24:30–31).

The Scriptures tell us that after receiving Holy Communion they immediately returned to Jerusalem, walking over seven miles in the dark to share what had happened:

And they said to one another, "Did not our heart burn within us while He talked with us on the road, and while He opened the Scrip-tures to us?" So they rose up that very hour and returned to Jerusa-lem, and found the eleven and those *who were* with them gathered together, saying, "The Lord is risen indeed, and has appeared to Simon!" And they told about the things *that had happened* on the road, and how He was known to them in the breaking of bread. (Luke 24:32–35)

---

16   This phrasing is echoed in Luke 22:19, the verse from the Gospel that describes the Lord's institution of the Eucharist. "And He took bread, gave thanks and broke *it*, and gave *it* to them, saying, "This is My body which is given for you; do this in remembrance of Me."

It is important to note that the recognition of the risen Lord begins in the explanation of the Holy Scriptures, but it does not end there! The Eucharist, found in the Church, is needed to complete the disciples' understanding. The act of breaking bread found in Luke 22 and 24 is a reference to Holy Communion. "Break bread" appears again in the Acts of the Apostles 20:7. These Scriptures teach us that the apostles and members of the Church experienced and came to know the risen Lord Jesus on a Sunday, the first day of the week, through receiving the Holy Eucharist. This experience led to their continued gathering each Sunday to celebrate the Lord's Resurrection and to commune with Him in and through the Eucharist.[17]

The Eucharist continued to be celebrated weekly in the early Church. In the second century, in his *First Apology*, Justin Martyr described the Christian worship service to the Roman Emperor, Antoninus. The elements of the service—such as hymns, Scripture reading from the "Apostles' Memoirs," recitation of the Lord's Prayer, and the homily—will sound very familiar to Orthodox Christians today. Regarding this sacrament St. Justin wrote:

Having ended the prayers, we salute one another with a kiss. There is then brought to the president [presbyter or priest] of the brethren bread and a cup of wine mixed with water; and he taking them, gives praise and glory to the Father of the universe, through the name of the Son and of the Holy Ghost [Spirit], and offers thanks at considerable length for our being counted worthy to receive these things at His hands. And when he has concluded the

---

17 The experience at the empty Tomb became the basis for the Church's timing of the Divine Liturgy. The Scriptures tell us that the women who set out to anoint the Body of Jesus did so on "the first *day* of the week . . . while it was still dark" (John 20:1). Likewise, the Divine Liturgy is celebrated in the morning in prayerful imitation of this scriptural reality.

prayers and thanksgivings, all the people present express their assent by saying Amen.[18]

This practice of Holy Communion is the basis for what the Orthodox Church does each Sunday. It is awe-inspiring to consider that from the beginning of the Church until now, the celebration of the Lord's Resurrection has continued uninterrupted in the Divine Liturgy.

Links Between Scripture and Tradition

THERE ARE THOUSANDS OF EXAMPLES of how Holy Scripture forms the basis for what is done in the services and life of the Church. I have illustrated just two. The faithful repeat these actions, prayers, hymns, services, and traditions, which are based in the Bible. In time, these lessons from the Bible in the life of the Church lead to the incorporation of the Holy Scriptures into our lives, and the stories and teachings of Christ become our companions and guides.

Of course, I had read my Bible starting in my childhood, but my study of the Scriptures was episodic. I had not developed the rhythm of reading and praying through the Bible daily, and to be honest, there are still days and seasons where I am lacking this daily observance. Additionally, for a long time, I failed to make the connection between what I read in the Bible and the practices of the Church. Eventually, as I found one connection after another, I became fond of saying that Orthodox Christianity lacks an imagination. Rather, all we seem to do is incorporate the Bible into how we live, everything we teach, and all our prayers.

---

18   Justin Martyr, *First Apology*, "Chapter 65. Administration of the sacraments." https://www.newadvent.org/fathers/0126.htm.

So, we must learn the Scriptures, as I have discovered, to help us to make the essential connections between what we read in the Bible and what we believe and do in the Church. Moreover, understanding these links between Scripture and Church Tradition guards our hearts by ensuring that our Christian life does not become a mere reading of texts. Additionally, reading the Scriptures keeps us from going to Church while ignoring the Bible. In such a state, the danger arises of disconnecting what we *believe* and what we *do* from Holy Scripture. If this occurs, the Eucharist or a memorial can become a mere tradition, custom, or empty ritual. But when we combine the Scriptures with our life in the Church, we become like Cleopas, whose heart burned with living faith while walking with Jesus on the road.

Understanding the Scriptures Through the Church

BACK IN THE EARLY 2000S I was invited to teach New Testament and Early Christian Literature at a local Protestant college, Colorado Christian University (CCU). My lectures were well attended, and over time several students entered the Orthodox Church. This eventually led to my dismissal. Parents of the students who had entered Orthodoxy were fearful that the school had brought a heretic into their midst who was corrupting the souls of their children, and they complained to the dean of students.

To be clear, my goal was never to convert a single student to the Orthodox Church or to persuade them of its truths. Rather, the texts we studied and the interpretations I offered were life changing. This had nothing to do with me. Rather, students fell in love with the clarity and authenticity of what is familiar and natural to those in the Church—the Faith "which was once for all delivered to the saints" (Jude 1:3). What many of my students had come to realize was this: To read the text of the Holy Scriptures is one thing, but to understand what they mean and how they should be applied is another. This combination has accompanied those in the Church from the beginning. It is, in a word, the Church's inheritance.

This fact was brought home to me during my time at CCU when I was invited into one of the doctoral prep courses. I had been asked to give a guest lecture to students who were preparing to enter theological studies at the highest level. The topic I was given was the unity of the Faith within Orthodoxy. The professor who taught the course was intrigued by what he understood to be the "so-called" claims of the Orthodox Church about its unified theological witness and practice through history.[19]

I began my lecture with an anecdote—an encounter that had occurred just a couple of years into my priesthood. I had written an article for our parish's monthly newsletter and afterward received a call from my bishop. He noticed a theological error and directed me to retract and correct my mistake. I was happy to make the correction, and in the following month, I did just that. I shared this story because I thought it was helpful and would demonstrate how even to this day the authority of the Church over and above any one person or priest is essential in order to guard the purity of the Faith. I also hoped that this example would show that this practice of letter writing by bishops today is similar to that found in the epistles of the New Testament, and also that a hierarch who oversees the local church is essential to a unified theology and practice.[20]

Anyway, before I was able to make another point from my presentation, an uproar ensued. Immediately, several students raised

---

19   This small section on Holy Scripture is not a detailed analysis of Orthodox theology and practice. It is also not an attempt to delve into the history and arguments for the Church's claims to be the One True Church.

20   Today we can read the letters of Ss. Peter and Paul as well as Ss. James and John and those of their successors, St. Polycarp and St. Clement. When we do, we find that from the time of the apostles to this present day, the Church has kept the Faith unchanged.

their hands and voices, wondering why I did not stand up for my theological views and why I didn't argue for the points I had made in my article. They wanted to know why I so easily caved in and did what this bishop asked me to do. To be honest, I was at first confused by their reactions. Then it dawned on me that my response to the bishop was in direct opposition to what these students were attempting to do through their studies. This came out as soon as the students began to express their positions. They felt that a true and authentic theologian should strike out and chart an original path when it came to expressing one's own view of things.

"Why would you listen to your bishop? Why conform to an established understanding? Don't you have a backbone? Shouldn't someone stand up for themselves and stick to their position?" These were some of the questions they asked.

Eventually, I had to explain to them that charting a personal course and defending one's interpretations against that of the received understanding was not "how theology should be done." It is not wise to follow one's own path when it comes to interpreting the Bible. Rather, it is my goal *not* to be original. I want to preach and teach only what was taught by Christ, preached by the apostles, and guarded by the Fathers and saints who followed the Twelve who followed Christ (John 20:21). I went on to explain to them that interpretation is something revealed to us by God and kept in His Church. Saint Paul wrote as much when he said, "These things I write to you, though I hope to come to you shortly; but if I am delayed, *I write* so that you may know how you ought to conduct yourself in the house of God, which is the church of the living God, the pillar and ground of the truth" (1 Tim. 3:14–15). The Apostle Paul taught that it is in the Church, which is the Body of Christ, that we find the lens through which we view the whole of Scripture. It is the Church that is the authority, not us.

Unfortunately, most of us have grown up in a world that views the texts of the Bible from differing perspectives. You could assemble Christians from various groups—Baptists, Methodists, non-denominationals, Roman Catholics, and Presbyterians—and while reading from the same text, come away with differing views. The same can be said of Christians within the same Christian denomination. Two Baptists may disagree on doctrine, as could two non-denominational Protestants.

To those outside of Christianity, this difference of teaching and interpretation poses a significant hurdle. How can Christians disagree about issues that they profess to be both central and fundamental to their faith? In response to this question, various solutions in the modern era have been proposed. But I suggest that we return to a more ancient concept, the original one: Correct interpretation and application of the Bible is found within the Church—specifically, the Orthodox Church. Moreover, no single interpretation is above that of the collective voice of the Body of Christ. Individuals should not attempt to promote their own views apart from the Church. Rather, it is spiritually wise to accept in humility what the Church offers us. This is what I was attempting to do in being obedient to my bishop.

The teaching we receive when we step into this living and original set of interpretations of the Orthodox Church connects us not only with the truths Christ revealed but with the body of believers who inhabit the Kingdom of God both in heaven and on earth. Moreover, like Chelsea hoped, when the apostolic teaching is lived out in the life of the Church, these truths of Holy Scripture are easily found in the local community that faithfully adheres to what God revealed. The Orthodox Church is not open to changing its interpretation to fit one person or the direction of the culture at a point in time. In a sense, the ground will not be shifting under an Orthodox Christian's feet. Instead, the stability of the Church's understanding and explanations is comforting and also timeless.

Life Transformation Through the Holy Scriptures

FOR ME ONE OF THE most terrifying things Jesus said was, "But why do you call Me 'Lord, Lord,' and not do the things which I say?" (Luke 6:46). Assimilating the words of Scripture into our lives is an absolute necessity.

When my children were younger, bedtime included reading them a story. Often this meant a child would end up in my lap or lying on my chest as I read to them. I distinctly remember reading a story to my daughter, Eleni, one evening. I was sitting on the floor next to her bed, and she was lying under her blanket. Not long after I began reading, she climbed off the bed and sat next to me. A few pages later she was in my lap, peering at the pages, and by the end of the book it felt like she was literally *in the story*.

This is a helpful example of the power of Holy Scripture. We can, by our constant and prayerful reading of it, enter into the story. This happens time and again in the hymns of the Church that are based in the stories of the Bible. Many of them move from a mere recounting of the events found in Scripture and jump to the first person. This means that in singing the hymns we too enter into and become part of the Scriptures, just as Eleni entered the bedtime story.

This is the point, though: We are to become scriptural. We are not just to study what we read; we are to be transformed by it. This clearly happened to Chelsea. She encountered truth, and it touched the deepest part of her. I remember another parishioner whose journey into Christianity was similar to hers. He came into the

Church from the world.[21] Slowly as he read the Bible and saw its application in the parish, he realized that not only was he changing, but he needed to continue changing by walking in obedience to Christ. So, when Christ says to love your enemies and bless those who curse you (Matt. 5:44), then that is what he is supposed to do.

Of course, incorporating these sayings of Christ is not easy, as anyone who has attempted to do so can attest. This is why the application of the Bible in our lives occurs within the supportive setting of Christ's Body, the Church. When St. Thomas questions the Resurrection, he does so outside of the community. We read in John 20:24 that Jesus appears to His disciples, but Thomas is not present. When he returns, the other disciples tell him that Jesus is risen. His response is famous: "Unless I see in His hands the print of the nails, and put my finger into the print of the nails, and put my hand into His side, I will not believe" (John 20:25b). One might think that the story would be more powerful if at that moment Jesus had appeared. Yet this is not what happens. Instead we read,

> And after eight days His disciples were again inside, and Thomas **with them** [emphasis mine]. Jesus came, the doors being shut, and stood in the midst, and said, "Peace to you!" Then He said to Thomas, "Reach your finger here, and look at My hands; and reach your hand *here*, and put *it* into My side. Do not be unbelieving, but believing." (John 20:26–27)

---

21 As St. John the beloved disciple taught, "Do not love the world or the things in the world. If anyone loves the world, the love of the Father is not in him. For all that *is* in the world—the lust of the flesh, the lust of the eyes, and the pride of life—is not of the Father but is of the world. And the world is passing away, and the lust of it; but he who does the will of God abides forever" (1 John 2:15–17).

Notice that Thomas spends eight days with his fellow disciples, and the description we get is that Thomas was "with them." This is a powerful reminder that living the Holy Scriptures requires help and a community around us who is also striving to live in faith. Faith and its outcomes are never the result of the belief that Christianity is "me, my Bible, and Jesus." Instead, incorporating the truths of Holy Scripture occurs in the company of others, for transformation does not take place when we are by ourselves.

Living the Scriptures, as we said, is hard. Assimilating the truths Christ taught is difficult, and transformation takes time. All of this is illustrated in the short passage above and in other places as well. We also see the difficulty of living a Christian life and our need for community in the lives of countless Christians through time. This is why we mentioned at the beginning of this chapter that going at it alone is unwise. If we hope to persist and succeed, we need to learn to bring our brokenness into the life of the Church. We need to trust in the rhythms of its life. These rhythms orient us toward what is beautiful and true. They heal us from a disordered way of life that alienates us from God and others.

I heard a story once about Fr. Thomas Hopko. I don't know if it is true or merely apocryphal. Someone told me that when Fr. Thomas left for college, his mother told him to promise her one thing.

"What is that, Mother?"

She said, "Go to church."

I can't imagine that Fr. Thomas's mother meant for this statement to be interpreted woodenly. I believe she knew what we need to learn—that applying the Scriptures to our lives and being transformed by them requires a personal commitment along with the gentle administrations of Jesus found in His Church.

Knowing Scripture Through Prayer and the Lives of the Saints

I JOKE WITH PEOPLE THAT no one goes to church more than me, but also that no one needs to go to church more than me. Without a doubt, the majority of my "knowledge" has come through living in the Church and going to church consistently. This is one of the ways we "read" our Bible. For example, the church services are full of biblical references. Each service is like a mini scripture lesson, if we pay attention to the hymns and prayers. Even the movements surrounding each of them provide insight. Additionally, the rhythms and customs of the Church serve the same purpose of increasing our understanding and application of the Holy Scriptures.

I remember preparing our paschal meals with my family when I was a young boy. My grandfather always purchased a lamb and prepared it while my grandmother, mother, and aunts baked sweet breads and dyed paschal eggs. The celebration and feast that ensued would begin right after the conclusion of the paschal vigil Liturgy, and it always felt as if the day was without end. We also celebrated in such a special and joyous way, there was no mistaking that this feast was unlike any other.

I am grateful to have experienced the positive changes in my life from a long association with the Bible *and* the Church. I have come a long way from my first days at seminary, when I asked Fr. Cleopas where his name came from. I can't help but smile when I think of how clueless I was about the Bible. Thankfully, my sense of what is in the Scripture today and how it is understood and applied is much deeper and more fulfilling. Thirty years ago I could not have imagined that learning the Scriptures would transform my life. I have seen this same transformation occur in others as well. It is a miracle how much growth can come through reading one's Bible.

I'd like to share two additional points of reflection before offering a few suggestions related to reading your Bible.[22]

1. *The best thing we can do is pray the Holy Scriptures.* This has been the practice throughout the life and history of the Church from the time of the apostles until today. We see this when we participate in the divine services of the Orthodox Church. These services (Matins, Vespers, Compline, Divine Liturgy, and others) are not a mere recitation or reading of the Scriptures but rather a praying of the Bible within the Body of Christ, the Church. In this sacred space and time, the gathered people of God come together and are led by Christ, who is the Head of the Church (Col. 1:15–20), together with the Father and the Holy Spirit. In God's Presence, we then pray *through* the Bible. Above any other means of learning Scripture is this life of prayer in the Church.[23] It is this corporate life of prayer that we try to imitate when we pray the Scriptures in our homes.

2. *The greatest commentaries and insights on Scripture come from the saints.* The saints are people who were committed unreservedly to a life in Christ within the Church. They adhered to God's revelation, prayed, fasted, shared what they had with the poor, practiced the commandments of Christ, were ascetical, lived a liturgical and sacramental life, and were often martyred.[24] The sanctity of their lives becomes appar-

---

22 Certainly, there are so many additional topics that could be covered, but this chapter is meant to be simple and introductory, nothing more.

23 Before we had a written Bible that contained the books of the New Testament, we had the Church. It was the Church that offered the Holy Scriptures to the people of God in the worship and sacraments.

24 Although many saints were highly educated, many were not. This lack of a formal education did not keep those saints from becoming devout followers of Jesus, nor did it keep them from developing remarkable insights into

ent to those who meet them, and in time it is recognized by the Church.

I am reminded of the story of a classmate of mine who went to Mount Athos, a monastic republic outside of Thessaloniki, Greece, in the hopes of meeting a revered elder named Paisios. After a few days, with his pilgrimage coming to an end, he was preparing to leave the monastery where he was staying. Before his departure, a monk approached him to wish him well on his journey and to inquire about his visit.

"Was your trip successful?"

"No," my classmate replied. "I came here with one purpose in mind, to meet Paisios."

"Oh," the monk said, "but you just did."

"When?!" my classmate replied.

"Just a few moments ago. The elderly monk who spoke with you at the well—that was Paisios."

Upon returning to the United States, my friend told me of this encounter. He explained to me that when he met St. Paisios (who was canonized by the Church on January 13, 2015), the thought occurred to him that he was meeting for the first time in his life *a true human being*. This feeling stayed with him for the rest of his trip and has until this day.

This encounter is similar to what others have experienced when meeting a saint. They meet someone who has been made whole, holy, and human by their long association with Christ through the Holy Scriptures in the life of the Church. It is from this space of sanctity that the saints serve us by applying what they have

---

the spiritual life and the human condition. From the time of the apostles, the Church has not shown preference for education over holiness; rather, sanctity is the true mark of spiritual maturity.

acquired from their spiritual efforts to lead us closer to God and His Kingdom. It is their example we try to imitate. These friends of Christ provide another avenue for us to learn and apply the Scriptures. Their lives remind us what we will find when we live like them. Following their example of living within the rhythm of the teachings, traditions, and services of the Church, we too find a complete explanation of the Bible and how to live it. Thus, by getting to know the saints—by reading about their lives, asking for them to pray for us, and imitating their manner of life—another way opens for us to learn the Bible and apply it to our lives.[25]

Getting Started or Restarted

AT THE CENTER OF EVERY Orthodox church is the Bible. I mean this both literally and figuratively. The Bible is the center of our life in Christ and in His Body, the Church. In fact, in every Orthodox church throughout the world the Gospels are placed on the altar—the heart of the sanctuary—and the Church attempts in many ways to draw our attention toward placing the Bible first.

---

25 For some the Christian practice of asking a saint to pray for them is problematic, to say the least. However, Christians have been asking saints like Peter the Apostle and Mary the Mother of Jesus to pray for them since the beginnings of the Church. The practice of intercessory prayer is commonly understood as positive. Many Christians ask others to pray for them but simply draw the line at asking a saint, who is dead, for their prayers. In the view of the Church and according to Scripture, this perspective is incorrect. There are many places in the Bible that contradict the idea that the saints are dead and now have no part in the life of Christians on earth or in directing the Church. There are literally too many passages from Scripture to cite. But as you consider the following questions—Are the saints dead or alive? Do the saints cooperate with God not only while they live on earth but afterward as well?—I suggest reading the following passages: Matthew 22:23–33; Matthew 27:51–53; Luke 9:28–36; Philippians 1:19b–26; 2 Peter 1:12–15.

One example occurs each Sunday during Orthros when the Gospel book is brought out by the clergy and the people are then invited to come forward and kiss it reverently.

These physical cues remind us of a spiritual reality. We do not just place the Bible in the visible center of the life of the Church; we place it at the core of our spiritual lives. There is no saint of the Church who did not make this commitment to placing the Holy Scriptures first. They each set out to learn the Scriptures, often memorizing whole portions while making daily study of the Bible a priority. Of course, we need to imitate them no matter where we are in our journey as a Christian. The bottom line is that we should be reading our Bibles.

Now, whether we have read the Bible from cover to cover, stopped reading it, or never opened the Scriptures, just getting started or restarted is a key step.[26] The life-changing benefits that come from knowing the Holy Scriptures are inaccessible to us if we fail to take steps toward establishing the discipline of reading our Bible. More importantly, consistent study should lead to our daily application of what we learn. Just knowing what is in the Bible is never enough; it must become the guide to how we live in this world.

I hasten to add that nobody is perfect when it comes to reading the Bible. I have experienced periods of study and seasons when my reading has not been consistent. I often read passages and find them hard to understand or remember. It is also true that my experience when reading the Bible can be dry. I can find reading Scripture much like reading a list of items found in my food pantry. I

---

26 Several times I mention words like *learn, study, read,* and *know* when speaking about the Bible. These words are helpful but fail to capture the whole story when it comes to the Scriptures. Yes, we need to learn our Bible, study our Bible, read our Bible, and know what it contains. Yet, these words can never adequately describe the Church's entire approach to the Holy Scriptures.

share this in the hope of encouraging you and to be honest with you about the challenges we face when reading Holy Scripture.

It is also true that, like the experience Chelsea had when she first read the passage from First Corinthians, I am often moved to tears by what I read. In these moments, I find the message of the Bible life altering. One way I have thought about these positive and negative experiences of reading Scripture comes from my childhood. I was fortunate to grow up in a home where family dinners were an almost daily occurrence. Yet if you were to ask me if I could recall each meal, I would have to tell you, "No." Some suppers were ordinary (grilled cheese and canned tomato soup) and seemed to provide nothing more than the basic nutrition I needed. Yet other meals (my mother's homemade avgolemono soup with fresh bread) were memorable and felt like a feast. The important thing was that every day we had a meal together, and I ate.

Of course, if I had not eaten each day, I am sure my health would have suffered. The same can be said of the practice of reading our Bible. Sometimes when we read it, we simply take in some nourishment from God, while at other times the Holy Spirit will lay out a feast for us that we will never forget.[27] In either scenario, we must realize that if we fail to read each day, our spiritual health will decline. So, get started—or restarted—today.

Bible-Reading Plans and Other Ways to Learn Scripture

NONE OF US IS THE same as anyone else. Some will find it easy to sit quietly with attention and read our Bible. Others will find that

---

27   Interestingly, the instruction I received in seminary was to read the Gospel during the Liturgy without emphasizing any particular word or phrase. The professor, Fr. Alkiviadis Calivas, said it was important to leave any emphasis to the Holy Spirit and to avoid "directing" people toward any particular portion of the passage by our manner of reading it aloud.

we can hardly read a short passage before our attention begins to fade. Some of us will find it best to read in the morning, others at night. Some of us will read in bed, others in our cars parked outside of work, and some in the middle of the day at a table with some tea. Still others may find reading almost impossible to do. For them, listening to the Bible or having someone read it to them is what will work best.

There are also several ways to learn what the Holy Scriptures teach. We might use a study guide, join a Bible study group, consult the commentaries of the Fathers of the Church, tune into a podcast, speak with our parish priest, listen to sermons, or purchase books that explain what is in the Bible.[28] We might read from a children's Bible at first, use the Orthodox Study Bible, learn Greek or Hebrew, utilize online resources, or follow a "read the Bible in a year" plan.[29] We may decide to focus on one book for a time or on a set of books like the Epistles of St. Paul, read the Parables of the New Testament, or learn to use a Psalter and begin praying the psalms daily. We could investigate the historical books of the Old Testament, delve into the Wisdom Literature

---

28 The Fathers of the Church are a group of early Christian theologians, bishops, writers, and saints whose proximity to the apostles and whose teachings on Christ and His life influence our understanding of the message of the Gospel. Examples of early Christian Fathers are St. John Chrysostom, St. Athanasius the Great, St. Justin the Martyr, Ss. Clement and Cyril of Alexandria, St. Basil the Great, and St. Gregory of Nyssa. Later Fathers of the Church include the saints Maximus the Confessor, John of Damascus, Symeon the New Theologian, and Gregory Palamas.

29 Of course, when choosing a resource, use some discernment and be careful to select materials that are trustworthy. It is important to choose first Orthodox sources—for example, commentaries on the Holy Scripture by the Church Fathers or books published by reliable Orthodox publishers. I think it is also important to note that the use of online material can be problematic. There is a lot of information online that is incorrect and misguided, and you may want to check with your priest before selecting a resource.

or search for keywords throughout the entirety of the Bible. Of course, if none of this makes sense to you right now, don't worry—you can also start at the first book in the Bible, Genesis, and go from there.

Now, in studying the Scriptures some of us will memorize what we read, others will copy out the Bible in longhand, some will learn to sing Bible verses, and parents may incorporate Bible stories into the stories they share with their children. (Yes, we should make a habit of reading to our children from the Bible.) Some may decide simply to read from their Bibles prayerfully as often as possible. The truth is, there is no limit when it comes to "learning" the Bible. I think it is best to take a "whatever works" approach to Scripture while keeping in mind what we have said thus far—especially those points about keeping intact our connection and interpretation of the Bible through the Church.

It is also true that having a reading plan can be beneficial. If you are familiar with the Orthodox Church and its lectionary—a set of readings associated with certain days, seasons, and feasts—then you may have realized that this method for reading Scriptures is a very ancient idea. For those of you who are wondering, you can find the lectionary of the Orthodox Church online in an app called "Daily Readings" or at your local Orthodox parish.

Some find using the lectionary helpful. For others, following it by themselves can be difficult. The reason for this is simple: The reading found on a specific day in the lectionary is associated with the liturgical calendar.[30] In practical terms, this means the readings

---

30   The liturgical calendar is both complex and simple. For our purposes, we will keep the explanation simple. As we go through the year, the Church has set up a rhythm that follows the life of Christ. The basic framework centers on about thirteen events from His life. Most of us know that on December 25 we celebrate Christmas, the Birth of Jesus, and that sometime

during the year may not follow a discernible pattern or even be in sequence with what came the day before. For example, if you happen to pick up the lectionary on August 29, you will find a series of readings associated with the commemoration of the beheading of St. John the Forerunner and Baptist of our Lord. However, the reading for the following day will not necessarily be connected to the Scriptures you read on the twenty-ninth.

Of course, reading the Scriptures of the day and allowing them to inform our sense of time and the rhythms of the liturgical year is extremely beneficial. One example of this is the set of readings that come before the fasting period of Great Lent: the Parable of the Publican and the Pharisee (Luke 18:10–14), the Parable of the Prodigal Son (Luke 15:11–32), the Parable of the Last Judgment (Matt. 25:31–46), and Christ's teachings on forgiveness (Matt. 6:14–21). Each of these readings—on humility, repentance, judgment, and forgiveness—prepares us to enter into the season of Lent.

In general, the Church uses specific readings from the Old and New Testaments to form our perspective and understanding of certain events in salvation history. However, because of the non-sequential way the lectionary can be laid out, it may not be best to read only from the lectionary. Instead, I encourage you to also read the Bible in a more concentrated and sequential way.

---

in the spring we celebrate Easter, known commonly in the Orthodox Church as Pascha—Christ's death and Resurrection. In addition, the liturgical calendar has other feasts that lay out the life of Christ for our reflection, and each of these feasts has a corresponding set of readings from the Bible. In addition, the liturgical calendar also commemorates certain saints of the Church who have modeled the Christian life. For example, each year on December 6 the Church remembers St. Nicholas of Myra. He was known for his generosity, and one event from his life is a basis for the tradition of giving gifts on Christmas Day.

A Suggested Approach

ONE APPROACH TO LEARNING THE Bible is to begin the discipline of Scripture reading with the Gospels (Matthew, Mark, Luke, and John) and to establish the pattern of reading them daily.[31] This pattern, once established, can be expanded to include other parts of the Bible. Keep in mind that even when reading the Bible in this way, the Church's view of the Scriptures is not segmented. Rather, we view the Holy Scriptures as a unified whole, even when we use a certain pattern or method for reading them.

Reading from the Gospel of Matthew and on through Mark, Luke, and John can be a beneficial starting point. This means you begin by reading chapter 1 of Matthew and continue reading until you complete the cycle of the four Gospels in John 21.[32] In total

---

31 Not long ago my daughter Maria asked me where she should start when reading her Bible. I reminded her that the first priority is the Gospels. "Start in Matthew," I told her. One reason for beginning with the Gospels is simple: In them we read about the life and ministry of Jesus Christ. He is the foundation of the entire Bible. Another way of saying this is that Jesus Christ is the lens through which we understand everything else in the Holy Scriptures. When I explain this to people, I usually remove my glasses and share that without them everything becomes blurry. But when I put them on, I can see the world around me with clarity.

   To a degree this reasoning is found also in the liturgical life of the Church. In the services we read through the Bible in cycles. Yet these cycles have a hierarchy to them, with the Gospels being first and the most important. This is apparent when we notice that it is the Gospels that are placed on the altar table, and only the clergy read the Gospels in the Divine Liturgy, often from the altar or just outside of it. In contrast, the Book of Acts and other books of the New Testament, as well as those from the Old Testament, are not read from this place of prominence. Typically a layperson reads them aloud from the reader's stand.

32 In general, I recommend that people begin reading from the Orthodox Study Bible. This is a convenient and easy way to learn the meaning of particular passages. A study Bible provides notes and interpretation as a companion to the text, and these notes in the Orthodox Study Bible, found at the bottom of each page, are written from the perspective of the ancient Church.

that is eighty-nine chapters: twenty-eight in Matthew, sixteen in Mark, twenty-four in Luke, and twenty-one in John. If you read a chapter a day, in approximately three months you will finish all four Gospels.

Now, if you are wondering what to do next, let me tell you this plainly: Start over in Matthew. Yes, that's right—after you read all four Gospels, go back to Matthew, chapter 1, and start the cycle again.[33] It's a good idea to repeat this cycle until the end of your life.

You may wonder why I place this lifelong cycle of Gospel readings first. The answer is simple: The Gospels tell us about Jesus. In them we learn about His life and His teachings. He is "the way, the truth, and the life" (John 14:6). By reading about Jesus Christ every day, our own life is reoriented around Him and His truths, and His way becomes ours as well.

Next, once this pattern of reading the Gospels every day is established, I recommend you add a second cycle. Begin by reading in Acts, chapter 1, and continue reading through Revelation 22. This is a much larger cycle of 171 chapters. Reading a chapter a day will get you through this portion of the Bible in about six months.

The third pattern you can add is from the Old Testament. At this stage your daily reading would include a chapter a day from the Old Testament as well as two from the New Testament. There are over a thousand chapters in the Old Testament, so by reading a chapter a day, you can get through the text in a few years.

Certainly, you do not need to stick to reading just one, two, or even three chapters a day from the Gospels, Acts to Revelation, or

---

33   I joke with people that they need to be "ABG Christians." ABG stands for "Always Be reading the Gospels."

from Genesis to Daniel.[34] Nor do you need to wait to start reading from all three, as I suggested above. Instead, you can start with all three and plan on reading several chapters a day from each of the three cycles mentioned. My only piece of advice is to stay consistent and be careful about attempting to do more than you are capable of sustaining. A mother of preschool children may struggle to complete even one chapter each day, while a retired engineer may be able to devote a lot of time to daily Bible study. Remember that in any stage of life, it can be better to read less with greater attention than to read much with distraction or with haste.

You will also notice a seasonality to your reading. You will experience times when reading the Holy Scriptures is easier as well as seasons when just reading one chapter will seem like moving a boulder up a hill. Nonetheless, the three cycles suggested here—the Gospels, Acts through Revelation, and the Old Testament—are just one pattern you can follow when it comes to a daily plan for reading your Bible. There are many others, including the lectionary of the Church.

Final Thoughts

ENCOUNTERING HOLY SCRIPTURE THROUGH THE eyes of someone like Chelsea is powerful. It reminds me of the Bible's ability to transform my own life. However, her transformation, like mine, did not end that day in my office. Rather, it continues in the love we find in the local community that emulates God's teachings. It continues in the numerous ways the Church connects us constantly to the Scriptures. It continues in the understanding and interpretations

---

34 The Orthodox Old Testament contains more books than Protestant Bibles, and the order of the books places the minor prophets before the major prophets. This is why the Old Testament in Protestant Bibles ends with the Book of Malachi, but in Orthodox Bibles, the Book of Daniel is at the end.

brought forth in the life of the Church and through the Church's authority, which reshape and reorient us in this life. It continues in the way each member of the Church is called to assimilate and incorporate the Bible into their daily life.

Finally, our transformation continues in the prayers of the Church, which we pray at home, and the witness that the lives of the saints provide to all Christians who wish to enter God's Kingdom. I hope all of us will make the reading and study of our Bible a daily spiritual practice and, with tears of recognition and joy, step into the Way of Christ.

And they said to one another, "Did not our heart burn within us while He talked with us on the road, and while He opened the Scriptures to us?" (Luke 24:32).

CHAPTER TWO

Confession: Love Breaks Through

I LIVE BY A LAKE in northern Colorado, and my wife's favorite thing to do is to head to the beach on the eastern edge of the water to watch the sun set over the Rockies. The reflection on the lake mirrors the sky, and that has led to hundreds of photos. The truth is, my wife never seems to tire of another "sunset shot."

Often others will join us. One evening, a neighbor approached me and, knowing that I am a priest, blurted out, "I think the idea of confession is ridiculous! What need is there for confessing to someone your sins? Anyone can speak directly to God and receive forgiveness!"

Of course, my neighbor was right. Yet, his anger and ignorance blinded him to the fact that confession is more than listing your sins before God in secret while no one else listens. Years of priesthood have helped me understand the difference between someone looking for an answer and someone who is trying to make a point, so I didn't pursue a discussion.

Like my neighbor, most people don't understand confession. Making matters worse is the fact that there are plenty of stereotypes that depict both priests and this important spiritual tool in a negative light. Who hasn't seen a movie or television show that mocks confession, or at best simplifies confession to a formulaic recitation of "Bless me, Father, for I have sinned; it has been two years since my last confession"?

Complicating this is how many find the idea of confession unnecessary. Plenty of people have said to me, "Father, I don't need confession. It's not like I've killed anyone." Thankfully, in over twenty years in ministry, this statement has been true most of the time. Yet it misses the point.

Misconceptions About Confession

BURIED BENEATH THE BELIEF THAT confession is only for murderers is a set of misconceptions. There are generally three: the meaning and value of this sacrament, the understanding of what constitutes a sin, and how any sin can affect us.

Confession is not simply reserved for those who have committed some unthinkable sin like murder and now hope for absolution. It is also for those who struggle with common sins like ingratitude, which you might wrongly think could never put your soul in danger. The truth is that murdering someone can estrange us from God and one another, but so can our inability to be thankful. In confession we seek to address the whole array of soul sicknesses that disfigure who we are.

At the same time, many are suspicious of the very idea of sin. Today the word may feel outdated or unnecessary. This viewpoint may stem from our questioning the existence of good and evil, or seeing the teachings of Scripture and the Church as antiquated and narrow minded. Yet such a view of ourselves and of the world is not only wrong but harmful.

The truth is, every one of us sins, and all of us are sinners. Holy Scripture presents sin as a universal problem. Saint John put it this way: "If we say that we have no sin, we deceive ourselves, and the truth is not in us. If we confess our sins, He is faithful and just to forgive us *our* sins and to cleanse us from all unrighteousness" (1 John 1:8–9).

Moreover, the difference between good and evil is real.[35] It is not just a matter of one's perspective. The Prophet Isaiah wrote, "Woe to those who call evil good, and good evil; Who put darkness for light, and light for darkness; Who put bitter for sweet, and sweet for bitter!" (Is. 5:20). The Book of Proverbs also notes, "There is a way *that seems* right to a man, / But its end *is* the way of death" (14:12).

Christ's ministry redirects us away from sin and evil and toward what is beautiful and is our true nature. In so many places by both His words and His actions, we see a new vision for what it means to be truly human. Take, for example, what is written in Ecclesiastes 3:11a: "He has made everything beautiful in its time. Also He has put eternity in their hearts." Repentance and confession are about discovering that eternal beauty gifted to us by our loving Creator. They are about scraping off the sins, the imposed imperfections that result from sin, and the disfigured ideas of who we are.

Nevertheless, I can relate to how my neighbor feels about confession and to the array of emotions in those who feel this sacrament is unnecessary. First, as I already stated, my neighbor was right. Anyone can simply confess their sins to God without the aid of a priest. The Church, in fact, encourages us to do this every day. However, sometimes we need to confess with a priest present, and Jesus taught as much.

Confession Is Biblical

AFTER JESUS' RESURRECTION HE VISITED His disciples and gave to them the authority to forgive sins. Here is the account in the Gospel of John (20:19–23):

---

35 Many have written about the existence of good and evil. The point of this chapter is not to discuss the debate around this topic. Rather, it is important to understand good and evil when discussing the purpose and value of the Sacrament of Confession.

Then, the same day at evening, being the first *day* of the week, when the doors were shut where the disciples were assembled, for fear of the Jews, Jesus came and stood in the midst, and said to them, "Peace *be* with you." When He had said this, He showed them *His* hands and His side. Then the disciples were glad when they saw the Lord.

So Jesus said to them again, "Peace to you! As the Father has sent Me, I also send you." And when He had said this, He breathed on *them*, and said to them, "Receive the Holy Spirit. If you forgive the sins of any, they are forgiven them; if you retain the *sins* of any, they are retained."

There are several important elements to consider in this text. The first is the words of Jesus spoken to the disciples: "As the Father has sent Me, I also send you." The Greek here conveys a sense of being sent with authority and purpose. The disciples are not merely running errands for God but rather are commissioned and placed over those who have faith in Jesus Christ. The Lord is sending His disciples out into the world just as He was sent out by the Father to care for God's children. Moreover, this authority is sealed by the gift of the Holy Spirit: "He breathed on *them*, and said to them, 'Receive the Holy Spirit.'" The disciples are like Christ, anointed in the Spirit; the difference is that their gifting is by grace (a gift of the Lord). Finally, the reason for God's sending of them and anointing them in the Spirit was to give them the authority to forgive people of their sins: "If you forgive the sins of any, they are forgiven them."

This authority was passed on by the apostles to their successors by the laying on of hands (2 Tim. 1:6), and this apostolic ministry has continued to this day in the Church. For example, I was ordained by Metropolitan Isaiah, a direct successor to one of the Twelve Apostles. Originally, the apostles and their successors exercised this authority to loose and bind sin (see also Matt. 16:19;

46

18:18) in a communal setting within the Church. This meant that individual Christians would confess their sins publicly in front of the entire congregation. The basis for this practice can be found in James 5:16, "Confess *your* trespasses to one another, and pray for one another, that you may be healed. The effective, fervent prayer of a righteous man avails much."

Other members of the community would repeat this act of confession, and a presbyter then offered a prayer of repentance and reconciliation. In time, for both practical and pastoral reasons, this practice was changed. Instead of offering confession publicly, Christians were encouraged to offer their confession privately, and the priest would witness a confession on behalf of the community and by the authority of his apostolic succession.

To this day, the Orthodox Church follows this scriptural pattern for confessing one's sins. In fact, the prayer offered by the priest recalls the words of the Gospel of John. After a penitent confesses, on behalf of Christ and His Church the priest prays,

> My spiritual child, who have made your confession to my humble person: I, a humble sinner, have no power to forgive sins on earth; only God can do that; but, trusting in the divinely spoken words that were addressed to the Apostles after the Resurrection of our Lord Jesus Christ, which said, "If you pronounce forgiven the sins of any, they are forgiven them; and if you pronounce unforgiven the sins of any, they remain unforgiven," we are bold to say: Whatever you have related to my humble and lowly person, and whatever you have failed to say either from ignorance or from forgetfulness, whatever it may be, may God forgive you in this present age and in the age to come.[36]

---

36   Father Evagoras Constantinides, trans., *The Priest's Service Book*, 2nd ed. (Merrillville, IN: Greek Orthodox Archdiocese of America, 1997), 149.

In the end, confession is not reserved for murderers alone. Rather, all of us benefit from an honest evaluation of where we have fallen short and of how evil may have distorted the way we live—and who we are. In this chapter of the book, I hope to give a clearer picture of what confession is, how it helps us, and how it is a spiritual tool that not only is beneficial but leads to a life transfigured by Christ.

Confession Brings Healing

As I left college and began life after school, certain sins had a hold on me. A few years later when I felt in my heart a call to attend seminary, my older brother said something to me that was funny but true. I had told the family I was going to Boston to enroll at Holy Cross Greek Orthodox Seminary. In response to this news, he replied, "Well, I'll never kiss your hand."

For those who are not familiar with this custom, let me explain. In the Orthodox Church it is customary at various times to kiss the hand of a priest. It is an act that honors not the priest per se but the One the priest represents, Jesus Christ (Heb. 4:14). Nonetheless, my brother's statement was connected to his belief that a clergyman should be a worthy representative of Jesus. He should be above reproach and spiritually healthy (1 Tim. 3:1–7). Well, I was not above reproach, as my brother knew. Plenty of sins had sickened me, and there is no doubt that unless they were healed, I would be a poor representative of Christ. If my sins continued to rule me, I would possibly end up hurting others.

To be honest, how far I have come regarding my own spiritual well-being is a question only God can answer. I still have sins that need to be healed, yet I hope I am getting better and that I am recovering my true nature.

In his universal letter St. James writes, "Confess *your* trespasses to one another, and pray for one another, that you may be healed" (James 5:16). The New King James translation of the Greek word ἁμαρτίας (hamartias) is "trespasses." I prefer to translate hamartias as "sins." Regardless, hamartias is a Greek word that means "to miss the mark." This is a term used in archery. Imagine an archer who draws their bow, notches an arrow, takes aim, and then misses their target. It helps to think of sin in this context, as the passage below illustrates:

> After these things [Jesus] went out and saw a tax collector named Levi, sitting at the tax office. And He said to him, "Follow Me." So he left all, rose up, and followed Him.
>
> Then Levi gave Him a great feast in his own house. And there were a great number of tax collectors and others who sat down with them. And their scribes and the Pharisees complained against His disciples, saying, "Why do You eat and drink with tax collectors and sinners?"
>
> Jesus answered and said to them, "Those who are well have no need of a physician, but those who are sick. I have not come to call *the* righteous but sinners, to repentance." (Luke 5:27–32)

When we sin, we are missing the mark for what it means to live rightly, to be truly human, and to be our true self. Jesus came to heal us of our misguided way of living. That is why He uses the words *physician* and *sick* while mentioning repentance.

In my own life, I have often missed the mark. I have four children, and I have not always parented patiently and with love. Instead, I have abused my authority and spoken to them in anger. At other times, I have ignored the needs of those around me and remained focused on myself. These are just two examples of how I have missed the mark of what it means to be truly human.

Saint James used similar language. He wrote that the confessing of our sins paired with prayer heals us! "Confess *your* trespasses to one another, and pray for one another, that you may be healed" (James 5:16). This means confession is therapeutic, not punitive.[37] It is a grace-filled occurrence that leads to our becoming whole.[38] It is not just a listing of the things we have done wrong coupled with the hope that fessing up will somehow get us out of being punished. This is too narrow a view.

I can attest to the fact that confession has helped me become whole. It has led me to the realization that Christ desires a relationship with me. In a sense, He wants me to see myself through His eyes and allow myself to be loved by Him; because of this, I can also love others. I can also say that confession has helped to heal those I have been privileged to serve as a priest. Since the day I announced my decision to leave for seminary, I have gone to confession hundreds of times. Each confession has provided a bit of God's healing grace. I have also benefited from the wisdom provided by the counsel of my confessors.

I don't think the neighbor who spoke to me by the lake could envision confession as a tool for healing, and that is a shame. Many

---

37 It is important for us to remember that the Church does not believe in an angry god who is mad at us or a Santa Claus god who's looking over the naughty-or-nice list to determine which misbehaving children he can punish or reward. Rather, our God is the God who loves us, embraces us (Luke 15:20), and wants to heal us.

38 In the Gospels we read the following: "Therefore you shall be perfect, just as your Father in heaven is perfect" (Matt. 5:48). The Greek word used here for "perfect" is τέλειοι (tell-ee), which is derived from the Greek word τέλος (telos), meaning "end" or "completion." When we think of being perfect like God, it is best if we have the understanding of wholeness in mind.

years ago, a wise old priest told me that the confessional was one of the most powerful tools in his priestly toolkit. "Father Evan," he said, "never underestimate the grace and the power of a true confession. It can change a life and do more than a thousand well-prepared sermons."

Confession Brings About Something New and Beautiful

THERE IS A BEAUTIFUL TRADITION in Japan known as *kintsugi*, which is a method of repairing broken pottery and glass objects. If you search for images of Japanese kintsugi, you will see vessels that have been restored by mending the broken pieces with gold lacquer. The kintsugi process honors the history of the object and renews it, making it more beautiful than it was.

Something similar is at work in confession. Wrongly we can think of the process of sin and our repentance as magic. We might come to believe that through confession, our past will be erased. While it is true that God no longer remembers our sin once it is confessed (Heb. 8:12), we often do remember. You might say that the marks sin has left in our lives remain. But these marks are no longer open wounds; they are signs of healing and restoration.

In the Orthodox Tradition, the icon of the Resurrection of Jesus Christ depicts a victorious and risen Lord who still carries the marks of the Cross. This portrayal is true to the witness of Holy Scripture. In the Gospel of John we read that Jesus appeared to His disciples after His Resurrection, and He showed Thomas the mark of the nails and also His side, which had been pierced on the Cross (John 20:27).

Similarly, our life after our confession will still bear the marks of our sins. However, these wounds no longer indicate our brokenness but our restoration. This is like the repaired pottery in kintsugi. Furthermore, it could be said that our healing has refashioned us into something new and more beautiful than who we were in the past.[39]

Confession Is Not About Our Past

I DON'T REMEMBER HEARING ABOUT the Sacrament of Confession when I was growing up in the Church.[40] That doesn't mean it wasn't talked about; more likely, I wasn't paying attention. In fact, the first time I confessed was during a life-changing week at a summer camp when I was around thirteen.

The priest I confessed to, Fr. Dean, would become my first spiritual father, and for the rest of my teenage and college years I would periodically meet with him to discuss my spiritual life and confess my sins.[41]

---

39 Saint Paul explains this healing renewal in his Second Letter to the Corinthians: "Therefore we do not lose heart. Even though our outward man is perishing, yet the inward *man* is being renewed day by day. For our light affliction, which is but for a moment, is working for us a far more exceeding *and* eternal weight of glory, while we do not look at the things which are seen, but at the things which are not seen. For the things which are seen *are* temporary, but the things which are not seen *are* eternal" (2 Cor. 4:16–18). This idea is found also in Fyodor Dostoevsky's novel *The Idiot.*

40 The word used in the Church for what are often called sacraments is "mystery." Thus, the Sacrament of Confession might be called the Mystery of Confession. A mystery is something we can understand only in part, but it is also something that we learn a bit more about over time. This is true about forgiveness and confession. These spiritual tools are, to a degree, a mystery. We can never know all there is to know about them, but by practicing them we can grow in understanding.

41 I will talk about the meaning of a spiritual father later in this chapter. Suffice to say that a spiritual father or father confessor is someone we grow to respect and trust over time. We share our lives with him in an appropriate manner, and he seeks to help us along our way of growing in the likeness of Christ.

In my mid-twenties, right after marrying Stacy, I decided to give what some call a life confession.[42] By then, I had moved to Seattle, Washington. My connection with Fr. Dean had grown spotty—not through any fault of the priest, but through my own negligence when it came to my life as a Christian. Like all of us, I have gone through seasons of both spiritual growth and stagnation. During the years I lived in the Northwest, and during a period of spiritual renewal, the priest I confessed to was a younger man by the name of Fr. John.

The experience of offering a life confession changed my view of confession for the better. Until that point—probably like most people—I understood confession and the act of seeking forgiveness from God as a backward-looking exercise. It was remedial. It was a spiritual discipline that invited a review of my past. This meant confession was an opportunity to consider where I had messed up and what mistakes I had made. In that sense, it was exclusively focused on the past.

With this mindset, I prepared my first life confession. Meticulously—scrupulously, some might even say—I wrote out a list of every sin I could remember, beginning from my childhood. Needless to say, the list was long and tedious.

Having prepared myself, I scheduled an appointment with Fr. John, who served a midsized parish on Capitol Hill, close to where my wife and I lived on Queen Anne Hill. Sometime in August, I went to see Fr. John.

For those who may not have a picture of what confession looks like, let me describe what happens in an Orthodox church. It is different from the movie images of Catholic confession many of us have seen. We picture a priest sitting in a confessional box on

---

42 A life confession is an attempt to articulate our sins honestly and clearly from as far back as we can remember to the present day.

the side of the church listening to penitents who enter silently into the other side of the small, closet-like structure. Then a small panel slides back, and, veiled by a screen, the priest invites the sinner to reveal their secrets.

In the tradition of the Orthodox Church, confession is done face to face, with the priest and the penitent standing or sitting side by side, typically before an icon of Jesus Christ. Sometimes a Bible and the cross of our Lord is placed before the one who has come to confess. Often prayers are mixed with intimate conversation and a healthy dose of familiarity. Anonymity is not a prized hallmark of confession in the Orthodox Church.[43]

So, there I was in Seattle in the 1990s for my face-to-face confession on a hot August day. Because the church had no air-conditioning back then, it was quite warm inside the sanctuary. Moreover, an Orthodox priest usually hears confessions wearing his cassock (a black robe with tight-fitting sleeves), often a loose-fitting outer cassock called an εξωράσον (exorasson) with flowing sleeves, and the priestly stole (epitrachelion) around his neck.[44]

This traditional scenario for confession meant that Fr. John was a bit warmer than I was. After praying before the icon of Christ we sat down in the front pew, and I pulled out my very *long* list. Some twenty minutes or so into my monotonous and labored reading of my sins, he did what I felt was unforgivable at the time—he fell asleep!

---

43 In confession we are invited to be seen and to be known without secrets. When we hide our true selves, life becomes difficult and unbearable.

44 Though these vestments are typical, confessions are sometimes heard in a more casual way. Someone may "confess" without setting up an appointment or may do so in passing, which occurs more often than you may think.

Yes, the priest I was confessing *my life* to and with whom I was sharing my most shameful and intimate sins . . . fell asleep. He even started snoring.

Looking back, I like to joke about the experience when sharing it with others. I mean, what is the protocol when a priest falls asleep on you during confession? Do you wake him up—or maybe not? Do you rush through confessing the sins you are most ashamed of while he sleeps? And if so, does that count?

Anyway, after sitting there for a moment, I realized Fr. John was not going to be waking up anytime soon. So, I gently reached over and tugged on his robe. His head jerked back, his right leg shot forward, and he was instantly awake.

Sheepishly, he looked at me and said, "Evan, did I fall asleep?"

"Yes," I said, "you did, and to be honest, I am upset."

What Fr. John said next changed my view of confession from that day forward.

"Well, Evan," he said, "you were droning on and on about your sins, which I can tell seem pretty important to you. But, honestly—and this may be a surprise to you—I am not all that interested in them. In fact, I am waiting for you to end so we can talk about who you might become."

Time and again, people are shocked to find out that priests are not all that interested in their list of sins. Having heard confessions for nearly twenty years, I can attest to the fact that sin is boring! Truthfully, I have heard it all. While each person's confession is sacred and a moment of deep intimacy overseen by God's grace, their list of sins is similar to that of any other person who has confessed.

This is an important thing to realize: Sin is boring. It is the absence of life, and our disordered way of thinking has us assuming the opposite. Most believe goodness is boring and that sin—evil—is exciting. Well, this isn't true. Anyone who has experienced sin comes to find that it is unsatisfying. When we realize that sin is the absence of all that is true and beautiful, there isn't much left to it.

Connected to this is the reality that people worry about what a priest will think of them as they share their confession. Many who confess to me are certain that my opinion of them will change once I am privy to all their dirty little secrets. Nothing could be further from the truth.

Instead, I am constantly humbled by the courage people demonstrate in sharing their brokenness with me. It is a time of grace, and priests are honored to be a part of these holy moments. I often feel a sense of shame myself when I realize I lack the honesty and boldness my parishioners have when offering their confessions. In the end, I am left feeling a bit closer to the one who has confessed, and I am grateful that they are willing to work on themselves.[45]

So, I learned on that hot Seattle day that confession is not just about looking back into our past and rummaging around to dig up and expose our sins.[46] Confession is an opportunity to review our lives and give an account for how we have gone astray, but more

---

45 Many of us have experienced something similar. For example, when a friend confides in us, we may notice how this forms a deeper connection between us and them. It also raises the level of esteem we have for our friend because we have witnessed their honesty and humility.

46 As I alluded to earlier, the word *sin* must be recalibrated in our hearts and minds. A sin is best understood as a type of disfigurement or even an illness that inhibits us from becoming who God intended us to be. Sin enslaves us into an existence that is limited. "To repent is to awaken from the sleep of ignorance, to rediscover our soul, to gain the meaning and purpose of our lives by responding to the incomparable love of the One who is 'not' of this world, the One who 'demonstrates' His own love toward us. The focal point should not be our imperfection but the perfect love of Jesus, who is good and loves humankind." John Chryssavgis, *Soul Mending: The Art of Spiritual Direction* (Holy Cross Greek Orthodox Press, 2005), 1.

importantly, it is an opportunity to consider how we can move forward and who we can become. After all, reviewing where we have been is extremely helpful when it comes to sorting out where we want to go, because thinking critically about our past is the starting point for moving forward in a new way—a way no longer conditioned totally by our past.

Jesus Envisions a New Future for Us

IN THE SEVENTH CHAPTER OF the Gospel of Luke, a religious leader invites Jesus to eat in his home. Having arrived at the house of this Pharisee, Jesus sits down to eat. What happens next is surprising. A woman from that city who is known to be a sinner comes and stands at His feet and begins weeping.

Soon she begins to wash Jesus' feet with her tears and dry them with her hair, even kissing the Lord's feet. This shocks Jesus' host, a man named Simon. He couldn't believe Jesus would allow this notorious sinner to touch Him in this way, especially if He were a supposed prophet of God. Certainly, a messenger from God would know what type of woman this was before she ever touched him. But instead of recoiling, Jesus reads His host's thoughts:

Jesus . . . said to him, "Simon, I have something to say to you."

So he said, "Teacher, say it."

"There was a certain creditor who had two debtors. One owed five hundred denarii, and the other fifty. And when they had nothing with which to repay, he freely forgave them both. Tell Me, therefore, which of them will love him more?"

Simon answered and said, "I suppose the *one* whom he forgave more."

And He said to him, "You have rightly judged." Then He turned to the woman and said to Simon, "Do you see this woman?

I entered your house; you gave Me no water for My feet, but she has washed My feet with her tears and wiped *them* with the hair of her head. You gave Me no kiss, but this woman has not ceased to kiss My feet since the time I came in. You did not anoint My head with oil, but this woman has anointed My feet with fragrant oil. Therefore I say to you, her sins, which *are* many, are forgiven, for she loved much. But to whom little is forgiven, *the same* loves little."

Then He said to her, "Your sins are forgiven."

And those who sat at the table with Him began to say to themselves, "Who is this who even forgives sins?"

Then He said to the woman, "Your faith has saved you. Go in peace." (Luke 7:40b–50)

This important passage from Luke's Gospel illustrates powerfully the point I made earlier when recounting my life confession. This spiritual tool is not just about our past but about our future too.

You may not see it, but only one of the three involved that fateful day at Simon's house was like me—stuck in the past. It wasn't the woman or Jesus; it was the Pharisee. He couldn't envision anything different or new happening. In his mind, people like this woman would always be what they were, and the best she could hope for was to come to terms with the facts: She was a sinner, and that was the end of the story.

Sadly, Simon's conclusion was that certain people are beyond help. Thankfully, this is not the position of the Lord. For Him, what is possible is still probable. He had no desire to define this woman by her past or to keep her trapped in sins she already committed. Instead, He was open to a new future. Likewise, Jesus is open to a new future for all of us, despite our sins and our inability to see it.

The Gift of the Future

I LIKE TO THINK OF Simon's way of thinking as the heresy of "I am." Early in my priesthood I was sitting with a couple who were struggling with their marriage. In one of our sessions together the wife said to me, "Listen, Father, my husband isn't going to change. He is just a liar, and that is that!"

I was struck by the finality inherent in her comment. She had made her mind up. Her husband wasn't going to change. He was trapped by his past. Thankfully, I had the courage to challenge her conclusion.

"Look," I said, "I am not doubting that the situation you find yourself in is hard, and there are a number of reasons for you to think that your husband will never change. But," I added, "there is only one Person in creation who can state, 'I AM,' and that is God. The rest of us are in a state of becoming." I wanted her to understand that all human beings have the opportunity to be forgiven and to change. Each of us has the ability to become the person God has created us to be.

Of course, that could mean we are moving toward holiness by becoming more and more human through repentance, confession, and forgiveness, or we are becoming less human by moving away from God and one another. It is a fact of life that at any point in time, who we are depends on the path we are following inside our own hearts. Any situation can be a moment of either holiness or hell, depending on whether we are listening to Christ or not. When we will not listen to the Lord, we remain hard-hearted, refusing to look at our sins and confess them to seek forgiveness and a new beginning. So, I reminded her that while we're in this life, no one is stuck.[47]

---

47 The Scriptures teach us that repentance can occur only in this life. After we pass, that door is closed. One passage from the Bible illustrates this point

Returning to the passage in Luke 7, it wasn't the woman who was caught up in the past, even though I am sure that before encountering Jesus she had felt unable to overcome her history of hurts and abuse. Like many of us, she probably wondered when, if ever, she would be able to overcome the sins that continued to derail and disfigure her. It is also likely that those who knew her wondered the same.

But on that day, her actions tell us that while she felt the weight of her sins, she no longer would be defined by them. Sadly, in contrast, Simon the Pharisee couldn't see beyond this woman's former way of being. She was a sinner, period. His view is similar to our view of ourselves and others—like the wife who couldn't see her husband differently.

On the other hand, Jesus, like the woman, was not fixed in the past, and this is the point of the lesson He offers to Simon. Unlike this Pharisee, He could envision a different future for the woman weeping at His feet. He was able in the present moment to see the possibilities of who she could become, and the sins she had committed did not determine the days ahead of her.

In my confession with Fr. John, I discovered that my past was not my story. On that day I came to realize that it was not only possible but perhaps likely that I could become someone different, and maybe someone better. This is one of the greatest gifts of confession and forgiveness—the gift of the future.

A question I often ask my parishioners is "How many times do you have to get up after sinning?" The answer is "One more time than you have fallen." I often tell those who confess to me that the

---

clearly: Luke 16:19–31, the Parable of the Rich Man and Lazarus. The key verse is 26, which explains that for those who have passed from this life into the next, "there is a great gulf fixed, so that those who want to pass from here to you cannot, nor can those from there pass to us."

key difference between them and a saint is how quickly the saints repent and how quickly they get up after falling.

Another image I like to share is that of a mountain climber who ascends a tall mountain with the sun at their back. This mountain is their sin, and their back is to the light, God. As they reach the summit, they find that the climb and the goal of summiting is hollow. Thus they begin a descent on the other side of the mountain. As they descend, they do so now in the shadows. This descent may take a long period, and often through self-condemnation, which is destructive, they may remain on that shaded mountainside.[48] At some point, however, they need to begin the long walk out of the shadows and back into the light.

This process is much like that of the Prodigal Son in Luke 15:11–32, who, after coming to himself and realizing how his journey into a far country had separated him from the goodness of his father's home, begins the long walk home. This journey is long; he is without money, proper clothing, and sustenance. He is unwashed and smelly. Unlike many of us, though, the son does not give up, and he makes his way home. There his father's love receives him, and he confesses his sins.

That is how we break out of this heresy of "I am"—by realizing we are not any of our sins. Rather, my sin is a virus or parasite that can for a time find a home in me. Thankfully, with confession and the grace of God such a state is temporary. The correct view of sin is that it dwells in us, but it is foreign and not a part of who we are. This is an important realization.

---

48   Self-condemnation is an emotion that often leads nowhere. In condemning ourselves, we can become stuck like a couch potato, and though we may feel sorry for ourselves, this feeling typically does not lead to meaningful change. The appropriate response to sin is sorrow that leads to repentance. Saint Paul writes about this in 2 Corinthians 7:10: "For godly sorrow produces repentance *leading* to salvation, not to be regretted; but the sorrow of the world produces death."

Confession Is an Act of Love—Love Breaks Through

THERE IS NO DOUBT THAT the love I was shown by others as I was growing up changed me. I wouldn't say I was an "easy child." Rather, my mom would argue the exact opposite. Yet, how do you heal someone who is broken? The answer is love.

I remember one of my cousins asking my grandmother if she loved me more than she loved him.

"No," she replied, "I don't love Evan more than you, but sometimes Evan needs more love than you do, and at other times the same goes for you."

This was true, and my grandmother knew it. More than that, she knew that all sins are the result of a lack of love, and forgiveness is an act of love. We can define sin by saying it is a break in our relationship with God or another human being. Of course, the best remedy to avoid a break between us and someone else is love.

The Gospel teaches us the same. The sinful woman in Luke 7 responded to Jesus' unconditional love by loving in return and thus confessing. This is what we do when we turn away from a disfigured way of life toward one that is rightly ordered. Saint John the Beloved Disciple describes love in this same way:

> Beloved, let us love one another, for love is of God; and everyone who loves is born of God and knows God. He who does not love does not know God, for God is love. In this the love of God was manifested toward us, that God has sent His only begotten Son into the world, that we might live through Him. In this is love, not that we loved God, but that He loved us and sent His Son *to be* the propitiation for our sins. Beloved, if God so loved us, we also ought to love one another. (1 John 4:7–11)

Saint John puts it more succinctly just a few verses later when he writes, "We love Him because He first loved us" (1 John 4:19).

Love is the basis for our confession of sins. Sitting in a room as I did in Seattle so many years ago, writing out my lists of sins, was a start. But it wasn't enough. As I have come to learn—to a greater degree as the years have gone by—love is a much better motivation than obligation or obedience for wanting to stand before God and weep for my sins.

I should also say love is a much better reason to confess one's sins than fear is. I mention this because so many come to confess and seek God's forgiveness out of their fear of judgment and eternal separation from God and others. This fear can be helpful in a way, but it is an imperfect tool. Once again St. John says it best when he writes, "There is no fear in love; but perfect love casts out fear, because fear involves torment. But he who fears has not been made perfect in love" (1 John 4:18).

This is one of the key lessons I am learning. You see, asking for and then offering forgiveness go hand in hand. (This is something we will discuss later.) In the passage about the sinful woman we read, "'Therefore I say to you, her sins, which *are* many, are forgiven, for she loved much. But to whom little is forgiven, *the same* loves little.' Then He said to her, 'Your sins are forgiven'" (Luke 7:47–48). Jesus' words show that forgiveness and being forgiven are actions of love.

I like to think that this woman had confessed her sins many times, perhaps in the solitude of her home or heart. However, when she encountered love personified in Jesus, something changed and broke open for her. She was able to accept God's love and receive His forgiveness.

The mystery of confession is the same. So many people through the years have shared that the experience of coming before God in the sacred space of His Church is liberating. They walk in and see the beauty of His temple in the icons, in the fragrance of the incense, and in the stillness of the space. Waiting for them is Christ's representative, the priest. It is into that sacred space, which reminds us of the sinful woman's experience with Christ in Simon's house, that love finally breaks through. In that moment, the ever-present reality of God's love can reign.

Confession Is Freedom

AT MY PARISH IN LOVELAND, Colorado, I like to bring out a special icon each Lent. The icon depicts the raising of Jesus' friend Lazarus, a miracle recounted to us in the eleventh chapter of the Gospel of John. Two of my favorite verses from this story come near the end of the chapter. After telling those who accompanied Jesus to Lazarus's gravesite to roll away the stone from the door of the tomb, Jesus cries out, "Lazarus, come forth!" (John 11:43). What happens next is dramatic: "And he who had died came out bound hand and foot with graveclothes, and his face was wrapped with a cloth. Jesus said to them, 'Loose him, and let him go'" (John 11:44).

To illustrate this event in my parish, the icon that we display of the raising of Lazarus is wrapped with strips of cloth. Each week during Great Lent we remove one of the strips until the icon of the raising of Lazarus is unbound.[49] Next to this icon, I place resources for confession and a sign-up sheet for parishioners who wish to schedule a time to meet with me for this sacrament.

---

49 In the Orthodox Church, Great Lent ends on a Friday. That evening we celebrate the Vespers of the Raising of Lazarus, one of the great feasts of the Orthodox Church. The Church understands that in the raising of Lazarus a foreshadowing of our own resurrection occurs. This feast day is celebrated on the Saturday that precedes Palm Sunday, the feast of Jesus' triumphal entry into Jerusalem.

Of course, the raising of Lazarus confirms Jesus' power over death and looks ahead to His own Resurrection. Yet, it also illustrates the power Christ has to unbind the sinner. Through Jesus we can be set free. We don't have to be bound by sin and imprisoned in a pattern that literally sucks the life out of us!

Saint Paul tasted that freedom, and in his Letter to the Romans he writes about it. He lays out the experience of freedom Christians can know in chapter 6 and concludes,

> For when you were slaves of sin, you were free in regard to righteousness. What fruit did you have then in the things of which you are now ashamed? For the end of those things *is* death. But now having been set free from sin, and having become slaves of God, you have your fruit to holiness, and the end, everlasting life. For the wages of sin *is* death, but the gift of God *is* eternal life in Christ Jesus our Lord. (Rom. 6:20–23)

Confession is freedom. No one bound to a sin would call themselves free. For example, consider someone suffering from an addiction. Their desire for phone time, alcohol, marijuana, pornography, food, fame, money, sex, power, and other temptations imprisons them. What alcoholic rejoices in their constant need for a drink? What fruit does their alcoholism bring? Similarly, being bound to a device, ingratitude, anger, or resentment is the same. The reality is that we become trapped in whatever sin we serve. Habitual sins destroy our freedom and take away our ability to exercise our will freely.

You may not realize it, but the liberation of our will is one of the most highly prized spiritual goals. The Orthodox view of the Fall recognizes that the loss of our liberty, which is the loss of our ability to use our freedom rightly, is the beginning of sin. Saint Paul understood this problem, and this is what led him to write, "All things are lawful for me, but not all things are helpful; all things are lawful for me, but not all things edify. Let no one seek his own, but each one the other's *well-being*" (1 Cor. 10:23–24). Being able to do what I want, whenever I want to do it, seems like the epitome of freedom, but is it?

The irony is that in choosing to be constantly self-directed, we lose our freedom. That is why St. Paul encourages us to focus our freedom not on our own desires and wants but on others. Ultimately sin is a selfish act and one that involves an increasing loss of freedom over time.

> Then Jesus said to those Jews who believed Him, "If you abide in My word, you are My disciples indeed. And you shall know the truth, and the truth shall make you free."
>
> They answered Him, "We are Abraham's descendants, and have never been in bondage to anyone. How *can* You say, 'You will be made free'?"
>
> Jesus answered them, "Most assuredly, I say to you, whoever commits sin is a slave of sin. And a slave does not abide in the house forever, *but* a son abides forever. Therefore if the Son makes you free, you shall be free indeed." (John 8:31–36)

Jesus came to set us free, but freedom comes at a cost: obedience to what is holy and healing. Freedom is possible when we direct our will toward following the Way and the teachings of Jesus. As St. Paul wrote in Romans 6:16, "Do you not know that to whom you present yourselves slaves to obey, you are that one's slaves whom you obey, whether of sin *leading* to death, or of obedience *leading* to righteousness?"

Confession is a spiritual tool that restores our will and gives us back our freedom. In a passage of Scripture that has become well-known to Christians, St. Paul describes a life of freedom this way: "But the fruit of the Spirit is love, joy, peace, longsuffering, kindness, goodness, faithfulness, gentleness, self-control. Against such there is no law. And those *who are* Christ's have crucified the flesh with its passions and desires. If we live in the Spirit, let us also walk in the Spirit" (Gal. 5:22–25). If confession is practiced regularly over time, we find that an increasing measure of freedom returns to our decision making. Sins that entrapped us start to lose their allure and their appeal. In their absence, we recover ourselves.

One of the more dramatic depictions of freedom is the story of the Gadarene demoniac in Luke 8:26–39. This man had been possessed and bound by demons. After Jesus sets him free, the man who had formerly been bound, estranged from others, and naked has changed: "Then they went out to see what had happened, and came to Jesus, and found the man from whom the demons had departed, sitting at the feet of Jesus, clothed and in his right mind" (v. 35). The phrase "sitting at the feet of Jesus, clothed and in his right mind" could describe any one of us who has been set free by Christ.

My dear friend Fr. Tom often uses this same story of the demoniac in the confessional. He believes that the man's liberation is important and instructive. He argues that like the demoniac, we can lose our identity when sin occupies our lives. In a part of the story we have not yet examined, Fr. Tom likes to point out that Jesus asks a simple question of the possessed man: "What is your name?" The demoniac's answer is both terrifying and telling. "Legion," he replies (Luke 8:30b).

This one-word answer tells us so much about the condition of this man—specifically, how he had lost his identity. Because of the numerous demons that possessed him, this man could no longer say his name. Instead, evil had covered up who he was. This new identity was not original or correct. Rather, it led to a way of explaining who he was from the outside in instead of from the inside out.

This man was not "Legion." He was not the sum of the many demons that possessed him, and neither are we the sum of our sins. Christ seeks to liberate us from sin, and when we participate in this process together, we remove the false identity that has been applied. We are now free to return to being the person God created us to be.

Confession Is Not Done Alone

I AM FOND OF SAYING that there is only one thing you can do all by yourself, and that is go to hell. It may sound harsh, but that is what makes hell so terrifying and terrible. Imagine spending eternity by yourself. On the other hand, going to heaven is something we do together.

So, if hell is the absence of relationships, heaven is the opposite. Jesus once said, "Again I say to you that if two of you agree on earth concerning anything that they ask, it will be done for them by My Father in heaven. For where two or three are gathered together in My name, I am there in the midst of them" (Matt. 18:19–20). Jesus teaches that He is present when we gather together in His name.

Confession is no different. It is an act we do while in relationship with one another. Returning to the raising of Jesus' friend Lazarus, in some of my favorite verses from that story we see the importance of community. The first indication of this is at the gravesite: "Then Jesus . . . came to the tomb. It was a cave, and a stone lay against it. Jesus said, 'Take away the stone'" (John 11:38–39). The process of Lazarus's liberation begins with Jesus' invitation to Lazarus's community. The Lord asks those who are present to remove the stone.

The community's participation continues when "he who had died came out bound hand and foot with graveclothes, and his face was wrapped with a cloth. Jesus said to them, 'Loose him, and let him go'" (John 11:44). On that day Lazarus exited the tomb with those who loved him watching. As he stepped out of the grave still bound by the graveclothes, his friends unbound him. It was Jesus who invited them to participate in this unbinding.[50]

I mentioned earlier that the Church has always encouraged us to confess our sins directly to God. However, if we believe confession to be only an individual act, we miss so much of what God and Holy Scripture teach us. Such a view is not the whole story. Consider how Jesus entered the world and how He ministered. His actions were communal, and His coworkers were not mere stand-ins. Rather, they were honored friends and participants in communicating His love and grace.

The truth is, Jesus wants us to be part of His plan of salvation. You may recall the healing of the paralytic in Luke 5:17–20. The story illustrates this very point:

> Now it happened on a certain day, as He was teaching, that there were Pharisees and teachers of the law sitting by, who had come out of every town of Galilee, Judea, and Jerusalem. And the power of the Lord was *present* to heal them. Then behold, men brought on a bed a man who was paralyzed, whom they sought to bring in and lay before Him. And when they could not find how they might bring him in, because of the crowd, they went up on the housetop and let him down with *his* bed through the tiling into the midst before Jesus.

---

50   The first time I thought about Lazarus's story in this way came during a conversation with my dear friend Fr. Tom.

When He saw their faith, He said to him, "Man, your sins are forgiven you."

Like the raising of Lazarus, this story is rather dramatic. Imagine the scene. As Jesus is teaching, a paralyzed man's friends climb up onto the roof and take it apart, then lower him on his bed to Jesus. The Bible says that when Jesus saw *their faith*—that is, the faith of the friends of the paralyzed man—He forgave the sick man his sins! That is a powerful demonstration of community and of the importance of being with others.

Now, imagine the long walk to where Jesus was and the disappointment that probably arose when this man's friends realized the crowd was too large. There was no way to get their friend to the Lord. I wonder: Who thought of the idea to climb up on the roof and dismantle it? I hope we all have friends like this— friends who go to great lengths to make sure we can be forgiven by God.[51]

There are, of course, several passages from Holy Scripture like this, but one of them is essential to our understanding that confession is not something we do alone. This passage comes after Jesus Christ's death on the Cross and His Resurrection, and it is found in John 20:19–23:

Then, the same day at evening, being the first *day* of the week, when the doors were shut where the disciples were assembled, for fear of the Jews, Jesus came and stood in the midst, and said to them, "Peace *be* with you." When He had said this, He showed them

---

51   In a healthy parish community, confession is normal. It is not something just one or two people do. Rather, it is something we all participate in, and the example of others encourages us.

His hands and His side. Then the disciples were glad when they saw the Lord.

So Jesus said to them again, "Peace to you! As the Father has sent Me, I also send you." And when He had said this, He breathed on *them,* and said to them, "Receive the Holy Spirit. If **you forgive the sins of any, they are forgiven them** [emphasis mine]; if you retain the *sins* of any, they are retained."

This passage forms the basis of how the Church practices confession. We recognize that Jesus commissioned His disciples. He granted them authority to forgive sins in His name.[52] In offering the Holy Spirit to His disciples and then granting them the authority to forgive sins, Jesus ensures that the process of forgiveness and confession will not be something we have to do alone.

It is also true that after years of prayer, spiritual struggle, counsel, and study, many priests have learned a thing or two about Christian living. This means that, like an experienced physician, they can usually diagnose a sickness of the soul more quickly than the patient can. As a result, priests provide insight as well as therapy when confusion and sickness have prevailed in someone's life.

In the end, there is so little that we do best alone. This is certainly true of confession. It is helpful to have someone with us, helping us and providing a tangible reminder of God's love, wisdom, and desire to be in relationship with us.

We need to come to trust someone other than ourselves. This is a powerful antidote to sin. For when we stand with another, we are stronger than when we stand alone.

---

52   The priest says exactly this during the prayer he offers after someone has shared their confession.

Confession Is About Making Changes

ADMITTING OUR SINS IS ONLY one part of confession; what we do afterward is the second part. It is not enough to confess what we have "done wrong" and leave it at that.

At times, I have felt that people are taking advantage of me during the Mystery of Confession. In these cases, people use me and the sacrament in a manner that fails to bring about spiritual growth and transformation. They come to seek absolution without actually offering a confession of their sins.[53]

"Father," they will say, "just read the prayer of forgiveness over me."[54]

"Well," I tell them, "you first need to make your confession."

Sometimes they will, and when they do, it often goes something like this: "Okay, here it is. I've done it all—I've cheated, I've gossiped, I have told lies, I've drunk too much, stolen money." They list their sins as if they were reading them from some preapproved, generic, and impersonal list.

In such cases it is easy to tell that the person hasn't given much thought to what they've confessed. Their confession lacks remorse, consideration, or insight as to what they might do differently. In this vein, many spend time in their confessions blaming others. We must avoid this at all costs. Jesus warned us,

---

53   Some call the prayer that the priest reads over a penitent the Prayer of Absolution. The prayer communicates God's promise of forgiveness, and it is offered by an ordained priest under the authority of the Church and the priest's bishop. It is absolute in the sense that we understand God's forgiveness as a gift that cannot be earned. We believe and teach that it is God's love and His desire to offer forgiveness to the faithful through His Church and her priests.

54   The prayer of forgiveness is technically "read over" someone. What this means is that after someone confesses, it is traditional for them to kneel before the icon of Christ. The priest then places his stole (epitrachelion) and hand over their head and reads the prayer.

Judge not, that you be not judged. For with what judgment you judge, you will be judged; and with the measure you use, it will be measured back to you. And why do you look at the speck in your brother's eye, but do not consider the plank in your own eye? Or how can you say to your brother, "Let me remove the speck from your eye"; and look, a plank *is* in your own eye? Hypocrite! First remove the plank from your own eye, and then you will see clearly to remove the speck from your brother's eye. (Matt. 7:1–5)

Jesus was pretty clear that when it comes to rooting out sin, the starting place is ourselves. Energy devoted to sorting through other people's sins and mistakes is a waste of time and is also unfruitful.

Sadly, being misguided in our approach to confession can be true even for the spiritually mature or longtime Christian. Like those who treat their confession like a trip to get their teeth cleaned, some overlook the importance of preparing and also of working on themselves afterward.

Unfortunately, in my early years as a priest I didn't have enough experience or courage to guide people who are in this frame of mind. So, I usually just said "the prayer." In such instances, the person typically got up, looked at me, and said something like, "We good? I'm forgiven?"

"Yes," I would reply.

They often responded with, "Okay, then, see you later."

I never did.[55]

---

55 Of course, offering confession for those who do not yet understand its purpose and meaning is still valuable. It is a sacred responsibility of the Church to offer spiritual tools like this to those who come to us. We also believe that God's grace is real and effective despite our own ignorance or willful disobedience. At the same time, priests bear a responsibility to instruct and guide people. It is important that the sacraments are not abused.

In John chapter 8, the story of the woman caught in the very act of adultery is told. While she was in bed with a man who was not her husband, religious leaders burst into the bedroom and pulled her out of his embrace. They then force-march her to Jesus, and here is what ensues:

> The scribes and Pharisees brought to Him a woman caught in adultery. And when they had set her in the midst, they said to Him, "Teacher, this woman was caught in adultery, in the very act. Now Moses, in the law, commanded us that such should be stoned. But what do You say?" This they said, testing Him, that they might have *something* of which to accuse Him. But Jesus stooped down and wrote on the ground with *His* finger, as though He did not hear.
>
> So when they continued asking Him, He raised Himself up and said to them, "He who is without sin among you, let him throw a stone at her first." And again He stooped down and wrote on the ground. Then those who heard *it*, being convicted by *their* conscience, went out one by one, beginning with the oldest *even* to the last. And Jesus was left alone, and the woman standing in the midst. When Jesus had raised Himself up and saw no one but the woman, He said to her, "Woman, where are those accusers of yours? Has no one condemned you?"
>
> She said, "No one, Lord."
>
> And Jesus said to her, "Neither do I condemn you; go and sin no more." (John 8:3–11; see also John 5:14)

This story, like many in the Gospels, is about God's limitless forgiveness. It is also a story that reminds us to look first at our own sins while avoiding judging others. In this way it is like the verses found in Matthew 7:1–5 about removing the plank from our own eye, which I quoted earlier.

However, what we often overlook is the final part of the story, where Jesus pronounces forgiveness while counseling the woman to "go and sin no more." Jesus' expectation is that the gift of forgiveness will lead the woman to change her life.

Being responsible for who we become and the future that is in front of us is essential to the act of confession. As we said earlier, confession is not just about listing our sins and having a prayer read over us. In this shortsighted view, we become numb to our sin and, worse, oblivious to our responsibility to change. In a sense, such carelessness toward confession is like receiving a gift and failing to say "thank you."

So, what does our gratitude for forgiveness look like? It is simple, really. We show our gratitude in the corrections we make in light of the goodness of God. He wants us to make a plan and work on making changes. This plan does not need to be complex. Rather, we can set a few goals that will help us to overcome the sins we have confessed.

One path we can follow when making a spiritual plan is simple: We can take our confession and the sins we have listed and write out our confession in reverse. So, if we have noticed that we struggle with materialism, we can list generosity as a goal. To take this a step further, we can get specific about how we plan to go about fostering this virtue.

Another spiritual plan we can follow is to examine the New Testament for the teachings and commandments of Christ. There are hundreds of them in the Gospels, such as, "Judge not, that you be not judged" (Matt. 7:1). We can simply make a list of them and pick a few to work on. We might also consider the Beatitudes (Matt. 5:1–12; Luke 6:20–23) or the Ten Commandments (Ex. 20:2–17) as a starting point. The point is not what plan we follow but that we make one. Like most things in life, progress is not accidental. So, making a plan is important.[56]

Confession Is About Forgiving Others

WHEN WE PARTAKE IN THE Sacrament of Confession, we are, of course, seeking God's forgiveness for missing the mark in many areas of our lives. But, at the same time, we must forgive others. Jesus made clear the connection between God's forgiveness and our forgiveness of others when He taught His disciples the Lord's Prayer, which contains the following phrase: "And forgive us our debts [or, our trespasses] as we forgive our debtors [or, those who trespass against us]" (Matt. 6:12). This prayer reminds us that being forgiven requires us to forgive. To make His point clear, Jesus continued, "For if you forgive men their trespasses, your heavenly Father will also forgive you. But if you do not forgive men their trespasses, neither will your Father forgive your trespasses" (Matt. 6:14–15).

One of the most important lessons we can learn from confession is how to forgive. There isn't a month that goes by that someone doesn't ask me about forgiving others. This is, understandably, one of the most difficult things God asks of us.

Of course, there is a difference between forgiving someone who cuts us off while we are driving and forgiving a close friend who betrays us or someone who abuses us. It is important not only to make this distinction but also to recognize the difference.

---

56   The Parable of the Unjust Steward, found in Luke 16:1–13, speaks to the importance of having a spiritual plan. In the parable, Jesus criticizes His followers, the sons of light, commenting that He wishes they were as shrewd as the sons of the world (16:9), who are astute in plans and schemes to obtain money. The sons of light, whose goal is the Kingdom of God, do not seem to be planning as carefully as they should to ensure that they might enter into eternal life.

Although it can be difficult, forgiving others is part of confession. In some ways, this begins as we prepare our confession (something we will talk about later). In reflecting prayerfully on our past and even about our aspirations, we may notice a connection between our sins, our hopes, and the actions of others. This connection might not be positive. Rather, we may find ourselves blaming others for our mistakes or even lessening the gravity of our sin by shifting responsibility to someone else.

In this time of reflection before confession, we can begin the process of forgiving others. This happens when we take responsibility for ourselves and our part in the sins we have committed. In saying this, I must quickly add that this does not mean we overlook or ignore abuse. It does not mean we remain in situations in which others harm us. Nor does it mean we ignore or gloss over the damage done by someone who acts in a dangerous or malevolent way. It doesn't even mean we shouldn't take positive actions to protect ourselves and others.[57]

However, we cannot spiritually heal and progress without eventually coming to a place of forgiveness. This is not only a gift we offer to someone else but a gift we give to ourselves. In many ways, the gift of forgiveness releases and unburdens us in a way that is transformative.

Forgiveness also very clearly connects us with the One who is all-merciful and forgiving. In our attempt to forgive, we approach God and become more like Him. We do something divine and find that this further liberates us from the sins we are prone to commit. This is what Jesus attempts to communicate to us in this incredible passage from the Gospel of Luke:

---

57   The topics of abuse and protecting ourselves and others are serious matters and beyond the scope of this chapter on confession. It is important to consult with your spiritual father about sorting through such issues.

But I say to you who hear: Love your enemies, do good to those who hate you, bless those who curse you, and pray for those who spitefully use you. To him who strikes you on the *one* cheek, offer the other also. And from him who takes away your cloak, do not withhold *your* tunic either. Give to everyone who asks of you. And from him who takes away your goods do not ask *them* back. And just as you want men to do to you, you also do to them likewise.

But if you love those who love you, what credit is that to you? For even sinners love those who love them. And if you do good to those who do good to you, what credit is that to you? For even sinners do the same. And if you lend *to those* from whom you hope to receive back, what credit is that to you? For even sinners lend to sinners to receive as much back. But love your enemies, do good, and lend, hoping for nothing in return; and your reward will be great, and you will be sons of the Most High. For He is kind to the unthankful and evil. Therefore be merciful, just as your Father also is merciful.

Judge not, and you shall not be judged. Condemn not, and you shall not be condemned. Forgive, and you will be forgiven. Give, and it will be given to you: good measure, pressed down, shaken together, and running over will be put into your bosom. For with the same measure that you use, it will be measured back to you. (Luke 6:27–38)

This work of forgiveness takes time and multiple attempts. The degree of hurt often determines the length of time and the number of tries it takes to forgive. But we can take comfort in the fact that God is patient with us and honors our intent. We may not get to a place where forgiveness overcomes our pain or we fully forgive, but the struggle should not keep us from the attempt.

How to Forgive

PEOPLE OFTEN ASK ME FOR help when it comes to forgiving others. They want to know how to move past their anger and hurt. And sometimes, the help of a spiritual father or a therapist may be needed.[58] With these caveats in mind, here are some steps we can take toward forgiving others.

1. *We should think carefully about what we want to do.*
   When a parishioner asks me about forgiving someone, I ask them, "Do you really want to forgive the person who hurt you?"

   Often people will immediately say, "Yes, of course I do. It is what Christ taught us!"

   At this stage I usually say something like, "Take a moment and prayerfully consider this point: Do you *really* want to forgive the other person?" This question is meant to help us clarify our will. What do we really want to do? Do we really want to let go of the hurt? You see, often the habits of holding on to the wrong and remembering past wounds become dear to us and feed our pride.

   In order to overcome a sin, we have to align our will with our spiritual goal. This is trickier than you might think, because we often have not done the preliminary work of checking ourselves and examining our intentions and will. Do we really want to put to death the sins of anger and unforgiveness, or do we "benefit" from the way that holding onto

---

58 The Church does not have a negative view of psychology, nor do we believe that talking about our past should be avoided in every situation. We know that much good can come from talking about and working through the hurts and offenses of our lives. In this section I am attempting to walk a fine line to distinguish a spiritual practice found in the teachings of Christ and how to apply it.

our hurt allows us to feel that we are in control and "justified"? This brings us to the next step.

2. *To forgive, we will have to address our pride.*
Forgiving others begins with combating the belief that "I am right, and the one who hurt me is wrong." The tricky part is that, actually, you may be in the right and the person who hurt you in the wrong. But in a spiritual sense, this does not matter. You see, deciding to forgive a wrong, even when we are right or justice is on our side, is a difficult but essential spiritual step. Sometimes I tell people that they can be right, or they can be in relationship. In other words, what is more important: the relationship or your pride? Of course, a healthy relationship includes the ability to work through difficult situations and the offenses that come, but spiritually healthy people seek first to put their pride in its place by setting it aside and focusing on the relationship. Consider the following passage in Matthew 5:23–24: "Therefore if you bring your gift to the altar, and there remember that your brother has something against you, leave your gift there before the altar, and go your way. First be reconciled to your brother, and then come and offer your gift." Note that Jesus doesn't mention who is at fault, but that there has been a break in relationship.

It is important to understand that forgiving someone doesn't guarantee a specific outcome. We sometimes think, "If I forgive, everything will be right again and our relationship will be healed!" This is not necessarily true. We should recall that God forgave us even as we remained separated from Him (Rom. 5:8). Nevertheless, forgiving others connects us with Christ and heals us. We do not forgive in order to force a particular result. Rather, we take this particular step with the knowledge that this is what Christ did.

In 2 Corinthians 5:21, St. Paul points out that Christ accepted our sin as His own: "For He made Him who knew no sin *to be* sin for us, that we might become the righteousness of God in Him." This is also what Christ did on the Cross; upon it He accepted the sin of the world (John 1:29) and refused to condemn those who crucified Him, even asking that God the Father forgive them (Luke 23:34). In our attempt to forgive, we are imitating Him and following His example and instruction.

At this point, we must exercise care. Applying this spiritual concept without careful consideration can be harmful. If our motives are wrong and our purpose is not clear, we will become stuck in bitterness.[59] Over time, while we attempt to forgive others, the feeling that we are simply letting them walk over us—like we are a doormat—will take over.

3. *In forgiving others, we first accept God's unmerited and unlimited mercy for us and then freely offer it.*
We can imagine God's forgiveness as a warm embrace or a comforting bath; thus bathed in the love of God, it becomes easier to offer the same to the person who hurt us.

There can be a type of spiritual sickness related to our pride that keeps us from offering love, mercy, and forgiveness to others. It shows up in our lives like the feelings of a hurt child who refuses to accept the love offered to them by their

---

59 We are forgiving others because we have decided to follow Christ's example and apply this spiritual concept in our lives. We do not forgive others because doing so makes us "better than" them; such an attitude will just stoke the embers of our vanity (which is another form of pride).

parent. When this occurs, we will continue to struggle to forgive. In this mindset we tend to view life and its challenges through the lens of justice instead of mercy. This can become an obsession, and we become fixated on the idea that those who have done us wrong must be held accountable.

Without first accepting mercy and God's forgiveness, we become stuck. We must remember that Christianity teaches us that mercy is more important than justice and if we fail to align ourselves with this spiritual law, forgiveness is unattainable, and in its place bitterness and anger take root and grow.

4. *We need to avoid talking about or reliving with others the wrongs done to us.*
Spiritually speaking, when we remember past offenses, we often become further entangled in our feelings of anger, bitterness, and injustice. This means that when we touch the hurts again and again by talking about them and reliving them in our mind, we become stuck in a world of resentment. Instead, we need to learn to lay down our hurt and move forward.[60]

5. *We must maintain our spiritual life during the journey of forgiveness.*
We can't look at forgiveness as a one-and-done spiritual exercise. Instead, by saying our prayers, fasting, giving alms, reading our Bibles, and attending services, we continue down

---

60   Once again, this does not mean we place ourselves in the path of danger. If someone has proven to be dangerous and unsafe, we take the appropriate steps to forgive them and to protect ourselves from further harm. Remember, God commanded us to love others, but He did not command us to trust or respect others; these last two qualities are earned over time.

the path of forgiveness.[61] It is helpful to look at forgiveness as a continuum. When we forgive someone, we are entering into the process of forgiving them, and our forgiveness should grow stronger over time.

6. *We need to participate in the communal life of the Church.*
It helps to have people around us who are also working toward forgiving others. It is inspiring to be surrounded by those who are striving to overcome sin and develop holiness. Having a community that supports us in forgiving, praying, fasting, and receiving the sacraments together as a body is essential.

Finally, note that the gift of forgiving others comes from an understanding of what we have been given. It finds its origin in being forgiven ourselves. This is clearly illustrated in Jesus' Parable of the Unmerciful Servant:

Then Peter came to Him and said, "Lord, how often shall my brother sin against me, and I forgive him? Up to seven times?"

Jesus said to him, "I do not say to you, up to seven times, but up to seventy times seven. Therefore the kingdom of heaven is like a certain king who wanted to settle accounts with his servants. And when he had begun to settle accounts, one was brought to him who owed him ten thousand talents. But as he was not able to pay, his master commanded that he be sold, with his wife and children and all that he had, and that payment be made. The servant therefore fell down before him, saying, 'Master, have patience with me, and I will pay you all.' Then the master of that servant was moved with compassion, released him, and forgave him the debt.

---

61   This is not all we do, but just a short list of a few spiritual practices.

"But that servant went out and found one of his fellow servants who owed him a hundred denarii; and he laid hands on him and took *him* by the throat, saying, 'Pay me what you owe!' So his fellow servant fell down at his feet and begged him, saying, 'Have patience with me, and I will pay you all.' And he would not, but went and threw him into prison till he should pay the debt. So when his fellow servants saw what had been done, they were very grieved, and came and told their master all that had been done. Then his master, after he had called him, said to him, 'You wicked servant! I forgave you all that debt because you begged me. Should you not also have had compassion on your fellow servant, just as I had pity on you?' And his master was angry, and delivered him to the torturers until he should pay all that was due to him.

"So My heavenly Father also will do to you if each of you, from his heart, does not forgive his brother his trespasses." (Matt. 18:21–35)

Here is the truth about forgiveness: It is based in our recognition of God's unconditional love and mercy. As we noted in the third step, when we understand this, it becomes easier to offer the same to others.

I should mention here that people often tell me that their frequent participation in the Sacrament of Confession has helped them along the path of forgiveness. What they mean is this: Coming to and conversing with God in the presence of a priest has instilled in them a new ability to forgive others. This sacrament, when frequent, predisposes us to forgiveness; in a sense, we learn the language of forgiveness, whereas an infrequent confession keeps us from practicing this essential spiritual discipline.

Humility and Obedience

NOTHING WORKS IN OUR SPIRITUAL life when pride dominates us. When we see ourselves as needing to be the center of attention, or as deserving of any desire we might have, pride has taken hold and directs our lives.

Once in the middle of the night, while staying at a monastery, a monk approached me after a service. He asked me if I wanted to know why I hadn't made any spiritual progress. Hesitantly, I replied, "Yes."

This was his prophetic answer: "Father Evan," he said, "the reason you are not making any progress is simple. You lack humility and obedience."

After this monk disappeared into the night, I walked alone the rest of the way to the small room where I was staying. Along the way, I began to think, "How dare he say I am not humble or obedient? What does he know about me and my spiritual progress?" Soon the realization dawned on me of just how prideful I am and of the extreme lack of humility that accompanies my Christian walk.

The Church reminds us of the importance of humility before we make our way into Great Lent. Each year the Church reads to us from the Parable of the Publican and the Pharisee (Luke 18:9–14), announcing our entry into this essential and important liturgical season. In Great Lent we attempt to grow more like Christ by increasing our time of prayer, fasting, and almsgiving.[62] Not only do we practice these three core spiritual disciplines with greater attention, but we read the Holy Scriptures with greater diligence, attend an increased number of church services, go on pilgrimages, and spend time reading spiritual works.

However, this passage of Scripture from Luke warns us that all our efforts will be fruitless if we lack humility:

---

62   I wrote about these disciplines in my first book, *Toolkit for Spiritual Growth: A Practical Guide to Prayer, Fasting, and Almsgiving.*

Also He spoke this parable to some who trusted in themselves that they were righteous, and despised others: "Two men went up to the temple to pray, one a Pharisee and the other a tax collector. The Pharisee stood and prayed thus with himself, 'God, I thank You that I am not like other men—extortioners, unjust, adulterers, or even as this tax collector. I fast twice a week; I give tithes of all that I possess.' And the tax collector, standing afar off, would not so much as raise *his* eyes to heaven, but beat his breast, saying, 'God, be merciful to me a sinner!' I tell you, this man went down to his house justified *rather* than the other; for everyone who exalts himself will be humbled, and he who humbles himself will be exalted." (Luke 18:9–14)

Likewise, in confession we are invited to humble ourselves. If we do so, our confessions become sweet and gentle. In this spiritual state, we notice a lack of resistance in ourselves toward God and the counsel He provides through Holy Scriptures, the Church, the priest, and the Holy Spirit who accompanies us in our confession.

When it comes to thinking about humility, I find myself looking also at the Parable of the Prodigal Son. It seems as if this teaching of Jesus has countless lessons for us, and one of them is about humility. You may recall that in the story, the younger son eventually returns to his father's home. I am struck by the fact that his trip home begins in a faraway country. There he has squandered the inheritance his father gave him, and in that impoverished state he finds a job on a pig farm. Feeding swine for work was a drastic change from the way he grew up on an estate with servants.

Eventually, though, he comes to himself while offering bean pods to pigs, realizing that the workers back at his father's home have it better than he does. At that point, he decides to go home and ask his father if he will take him back, not as his son but as a servant. With this new humble view of himself, he begins the long walk home.

In thinking about this story, we don't often consider that his journey home took time. Moreover, it wasn't as if he changed his clothes, took a shower, packed his bag with some snacks, and found a ride. As I mentioned earlier, the smell of the pigs is on him, he is wearing tattered clothes covered in dried mud, and he walks with little or nothing to eat. He returns home debased and degraded.

During that walk, he has time to process how life has humbled him. Upon returning to his father's home, his dad unexpectedly embraces and welcomes him. What the son does next is surprising. He confesses his sins to his father in the presence of the servants who previously served him, saying, "Father, I have sinned against heaven and in your sight, and am no longer worthy to be called your son" (Luke 15:21).

I am not sure whether he had intended to make his confession not only to his father but also in front of the servants when he came to himself days earlier in the pigpen. Yet the walk, his circumstances, and the love his father showed him worked together to develop the seed of humility that had been planted in his heart.

Can we imagine confessing our sins in the presence of others— let alone people who used to be our servants? At first, probably not, but this is what humility does: It makes us courageous and fearless when it comes to facing sin. We see in the Prodigal Son a path we too must follow.

Humility is very important, and this story reminds us that when it accompanies our confession, we are transformed. In the story the son is first humiliated and only later comes to accept his humble state—his humiliation. This must become true for us as well. We need to go through a similar process.

Returning to the advice I received at the monastery, the monk noticed that I not only lacked humility but that I also lacked obedience. Even now the realization that the teachings of Jesus have not penetrated my actions often accompanies me when I prepare my confession. Like you, I read in Holy Scripture what He teaches but then fail to put it into practice.

We have to understand that obedience is not a dirty word but rather an overlooked one. We need obedience if we hope to be transformed. Without it, we find ourselves stuck in an unending cycle of sin.

Thankfully, obedience to God is light and peaceful when humility is formed first inside our hearts. This is why the monk placed humility first in the list of things keeping me from progressing spiritually. This is also why any attempt at obedience is doomed to fail when pride is at work in us.

Jesus assured us: "Take My yoke upon you and learn from Me, for I am gentle and lowly in heart, and you will find rest for your souls. For My yoke *is* easy and My burden is light" (Matt. 11:29–30). This passage effortlessly mingles humility with the concept of obedience. In such a spirit, the challenges we encounter because of sin do not lead us toward despondency, which is a type of spiritual depression. Rather, because of humility coupled with obedience, we can address sin with patience, knowing that these two spiritual tools make it possible to be transformed for the better.

It is also important to recognize that as we acquire humility and obedience, our relationships with those around us change. Our interactions with family members, friends, coworkers, strangers, and enemies improve. We no longer have to be first, right, critical of others, or self-seeking. Instead, we can, in a spirit of humility and obedience, leave space for others while lessening the area we occupy.

Practical Steps for Confession

IN MY WORK IN THE parish, I spend time explaining the meaning, or theology, of confession. However, people also want to know how to find someone to confess to, how to prepare themselves, what will happen, and other important details. Here are some steps to take, followed by a series of questions and short answers that I hope you will find helpful.

CHOOSE A PRIEST

CONFESSING TO SOMEONE YOU HAVE grown to trust is important. Trust is built up over time and is based in mutual freedom, respect, and love. In this setting, one can be appropriately vulnerable and intimate about their life and sins.[63]

Of course, the level of maturity and expertise of a priest will vary, and you should remember that not all priests can hear confessions.[64] So, make sure to ask him if he has a blessing to do so, and be discerning in choosing a father confessor.

---

63 I want to emphasize the importance of appropriate vulnerability and intimacy. Abuse can occur in both the penitent and the confessor. We should be careful to share only what is necessary and appropriate in our confession. Intimate personal details such as names and dates are usually unnecessary and may be a sign that the relationship has become unhealthy. Similarly, mutual freedom, respect, and love should always be part of the relationship. Confessions should never occur under forced obedience, compulsion, or coercion. Likewise, respect for one another and Christian love are essential. Let me also say that we should not set aside common sense or our personal boundaries when navigating a relationship with a priest. It is not appropriate for a priest to snoop, pry, or investigate. Nor should a priest or a penitent seek to give or get direction for every decision or circumstance.

64 The responsibility and privilege of hearing confessions is granted by a priest's local bishop. It is common for a bishop to wait until a priest has demonstrated both spiritual maturity and a level of discernment before he allows him to hear confessions.

When a priest is given the responsibility of hearing confessions, regardless of his education or experience, he offers the grace of Christ by virtue of his ordination. In the end, the One True Priest is Jesus Christ. Every priest on earth is a representative of Him, and all authority, grace, and wisdom come from Him regardless of the priest we encounter.

Now, finding someone to confess to is usually as simple as approaching your local parish priest.[65] However, if there are several priests nearby, you may decide to speak with them all before choosing one.

Once you find a priest to confess to, give yourself a bit of time to get used to one another. Keep in mind that you are not required to remain with the same priest forever. Nor is he required to keep you as a spiritual child.[66] At the same time, you shouldn't move from one priest to another frequently. If possible, and if the relationship is healthy, keeping the same priest over time—or for a lifetime—is beneficial, just as keeping the same physician is helpful.

It is also perfectly fine to confess to someone you don't have a close relationship with. If forming a bond with a local priest is not

---

65 The Sacrament of Confession should be done in person. Confessing your sins to one priest over the phone or in correspondence while seeking the prayers of reconciliation (absolution) from a different priest is not a best practice and should be avoided.

66 Some are uncomfortable with the terms *spiritual father* and *spiritual child*. Nonetheless, these terms are found in Holy Scripture. Saint Paul was a spiritual father to Timothy and Titus, and they were spiritual sons of St. Paul, who wrote: "I do not write these things to shame you, but as my beloved children I warn *you*. For though you might have ten thousand instructors in Christ, yet *you do not have* many fathers; for in Christ Jesus I have begotten you through the gospel.... I have sent Timothy to you, who is my beloved and faithful son in the Lord, who will remind you of my ways in Christ, as I teach everywhere in every church" (1 Cor. 4:14–17; see also 1 Tim. 1:18 and Titus 1:4).

possible, this does not diminish the grace of this mystery of the Faith. The priest you confess to does not have to be the same priest you approach to seek spiritual advice and direction. Rather, properly preparing and offering your confession is beneficial, regardless of which priest you confess to.

If you are not particularly close to the priest you confess to, or you find that he is not in the best position to offer guidance, you can seek spiritual direction in many other ways. You can find a priest to correspond with and turn toward the Bible, the writings of the saints, and other spiritual works for direction. I should add here that it is not uncommon for people to forego confession because they haven't found the "perfect spiritual father." This is a mistake. Rather, we should confess our sins in the Sacrament of Confession and seek out spiritual counsel elsewhere.

Additionally, we should never underestimate the possibility that God's grace will break through during our confession, regardless of our confessor. I have experienced times when I have offered a confession to a priest whom I didn't know well or didn't have a great relationship with. Yet I still received a word or a message from God that helped me greatly.

PREPARE AHEAD OF TIME

BELIEVE IT OR NOT, CONFESSING our sins to a priest is not the best time to repent. Let me explain what I mean. Repentance is something that should occur prior to showing up to give our confession. In other words, the decision to confess comes after we realize that what we have done is sinful. Another way of saying this is that if we prepare ourselves properly for confession, repentance is a natural outcome. This happens when we review our life in light of the teachings of Christ. We come to see what is disfigured, and if we are moving in the right direction, godly sorrow will take hold of us.[67] This is a positive outcome, and unlike guilt, this sorrow leads us forward toward repentance and a changed lifestyle.[68]

During the process of repenting, some of us may shed tears when preparing our confession as we come to terms with the damage we have done to ourselves and others by our actions and inactions.[69]

---

67 Saint Paul writes, "For even if I made you sorry with my letter, I do not regret it; though I did regret it. For I perceive that the same epistle made you sorry, though only for a while. Now I rejoice, not that you were made sorry, but that your sorrow led to repentance. For you were made sorry in a godly manner, that you might suffer loss from us in nothing. For godly sorrow produces repentance *leading* to salvation, not to be regretted; but the sorrow of the world produces death. For observe this very thing, that you sorrowed in a godly manner: What diligence it produced in you, *what* clearing *of yourselves, what* indignation, *what* fear, *what* vehement desire, *what* zeal, *what* vindication! In all *things* you proved yourselves to be clear in this matter. Therefore, although I wrote to you, *I did* not *do it* for the sake of him who had done the wrong, nor for the sake of him who suffered wrong, but that our care for you in the sight of God might appear to you" (2 Cor. 7:8–12).

68 I don't think guilt is a particularly helpful emotion or state. I would even go as far as to say guilt is not Christian, at least as it is commonly understood today. More often than not, guilt leaves us feeling sorry for ourselves and leads to self-condemnation and becoming stuck in our sins. On the other hand, godly sorrow is active, even if it is a bit painful. It is like sitting on a sharp needle; it pricks us and causes us to get up. Of course, understanding that sin leaves all of us short of the glory of God (Rom. 3:23) is essential to a correct Christian perspective about the impact of sins.

69 Gerondissa (now Saint) Gavrilia wrote, "I will tell you. The moment we become aware that we did something wrong, we shed tears, we shall feel contrition, we shall repent. Then the joy of pardon should follow, because we know that God is compassionate and all-merciful. Does anyone ever come out of confession crying? No. He cries while confessing, for his sins and all the wrong he did. But to come out and still cry, after having confessed? I don't accept that." Her interviewer said, "It means he did not really confess," and Gerondissa responded, "Correct!" Nun Gavrilia, *The Ascetic of Love*, tr. Helen Anthony (Sea Salt Books, 2022), 206.

It is true that we often fail to see our sins at first. The so-called big sins cloud our vision, or we have grown so accustomed to sin that we can't or don't notice what ails us. In this situation, a practical guide found in a prayer book can help. I still use one to this day, and there are many different versions available. The one I use encourages me to review my life by looking at the Beatitudes and the Ten Commandments. Lists of sins are also available that can help us focus on what we wish to confess. I have also found the confession written by St. John of Kronstadt particularly insightful in preparing my own. When using it I often rewrite it, including what is pertinent to my confession and omitting what is not. (I have included this resource on page 112.)

SET AN APPOINTMENT

SOMETIMES THE HARDEST PART OF confession is the decision to go. Countless times I have met with someone who said as much.[70] Often pride and shame keep us from stepping out of our hiding spot. This is nothing new. When Adam sinned in the Garden, his inclination was to hide. So it is with us, falling into the same pattern as our foreparent; we too seek to keep our sins hidden. Unfortunately, what remains hidden cannot be healed.

Once you have decided to confess, you should show up prepared. Take some time to think about what you wish to confess. I will talk a bit more about this below.

---

70 The customs and traditions around confession can vary greatly. In some parishes, confession is offered either before or as part of the daily office of prayer. This means someone can show up during Vespers or Orthros (Matins) and confess. In some parishes, parishioners need to set up an appointment, and in others both options are available.

When you show up to give your confession, you will typically meet the priest in the nave of the church and stand before the icon of Christ. The location can vary depending on the setup of the parish or the circumstances. (I have heard confessions in the hospital, on a mountainside, in people's homes, in my office, in a field, and once at the back of a plane on a flight to Boston.)

Additionally, the amount of time available to offer your confession will vary. Generally speaking, a thorough confession can be given in under five minutes, but there is certainly nothing wrong in taking more time.[71]

After you arrive, you may choose to seek the blessing of the priest and then go stand beside him before Christ.[72] It is typical to stand on his right. This physical arrangement mirrors what we read in the Gospel of Matthew (25:31–46) in the description of the Last Judgment: In this parable, the sheep of God, who represent the righteous, are standing at His right. This simple orientation conveys to us the immediacy of God's forgiveness and love. As Christ tells us in the Parable of the Prodigal Son, our loving

---

71   Recently I discussed this topic with an experienced, respected, and venerable father confessor, originally of Mount Athos, who is an abbot of a monastery here in America. He is often called upon to hear hundreds of confessions in various regions of North America, and he receives thousands of pilgrims who confess to him each year. He shared with me that the time of one's confession should be short—he advised under three minutes.

72   Receiving the blessing of a priest is customary when greeting him. To do so, simply place your right hand over your left with your palms facing up. It is then traditional to say to the priest, "Father, bless." In response, the priest offers the blessing of Christ. He will say, "The Lord bless you." A priest is a representative of Christ by virtue of his ordination. Priests do not offer their own blessing but Christ's. In doing so they form the letters "ICXC" with their right hand and make the sign of the cross over the person seeking a blessing. It is then customary to kiss the right hand of the priest.

Father hastens to embrace and kiss His lost son before he even speaks of his sins.

There, standing before the icon of Christ, the priest will offer the opening prayers of the sacrament. When he finishes, he will typically ask you to offer your confession. At this point, he may invite you to give your confession standing, kneeling, or even sitting down. When confessing, it is perfectly normal to pull out a list and read from it. You may also wish to share what is on your heart without referencing a list.

Even though you have prepared, you may find that offering a confession is nerve-wracking. You may get emotional, lose your train of thought, and find yourself with tears flowing. Not to worry; you can't do it wrong.

I like to gently remind parishioners that only two confessions are incorrect. The first goes like this: "Father, I don't have anything to confess. It's not like I've murdered anyone." The second is just as misguided: "Father, I have done it all." Both demonstrate a lack of preparation and a lack of an honest review of our lives. No one is without sin, and no one has committed every sin. The truth is somewhere in between, and offering a specific—even brief— confession is better than claiming "nothing" or "everything." Also, don't worry about getting it right or remembering everything. Just do your best. After you finish, the priest may wish to offer a word or two. Remember, your confession time is not always the space for a full pastoral counseling session.

The priest will then ask you to kneel—if you can't kneel, don't worry—and he will place the stole (epitrachelion) over your head while you face the icon of Christ. On top of the priestly stole, he places his right hand and then reads the prayer of forgiveness. (I have included this prayer on page 111.) Once this prayer is read, you will be invited to stand and depart.

Frequently Asked Questions

WHAT IS A SPIRITUAL FATHER?

The tradition of a spiritual father comes from Scripture and from the time-tested Tradition and life of the Church.[73] He is someone we trust and who occupies an important place in our spiritual life. A spiritual father is not a guru, nor should we expect that he has the gift of discernment—this gift is bestowed upon only a few by the Holy Spirit. Instead, we should expect spiritual fathers (and mothers) to be well formed spiritually, mature in judgment, and well versed in the Holy Scriptures and teachings of the Church.[74] They should be temperate and kind, exhibiting the qualities of Christ and the virtues of the Christian life. They can provide counsel and guidance, but this is not their full-time purpose. This means we should not expect them to guide and direct us in every matter. Yet, their spiritual advice, broadly speaking, should be carefully applied and considered.

Finally, there is no room in this relationship for coercion, manipulation, and abuse of any kind. (This goes both ways.) Moreover, a spiritual father should neither pry nor be taciturn. Rather, he should be straightforward and clear, keeping a proper disposition that is friendly but not overly so.

---

73 Saint Paul describes himself as a father to the people of Corinth: "For though you might have ten thousand instructors in Christ, yet *you do* not *have* many fathers; for in Christ Jesus I have begotten you through the gospel" (1 Cor. 4:15).

74 It is not unusual for a woman in the Church to fulfill a similar role. Typically, a spiritual mother is an abbess or a revered monastic. She functions in much the same way as a spiritual father, although she cannot offer the prayer of forgiveness as a priest does. I often refer women in my parish to an abbess I have come to respect and admire.

WHAT DO I ACTUALLY DO TO GET READY?

Begin by praying and asking God to open your heart and guide you. As I mentioned earlier, you may use a confession guide if you have one (included in many Orthodox prayer books) and write down what you wish to share. Your list does not need to be long or overly detailed. It is okay to be thematic and brief. Details should be offered only when necessary. For example, if you have struggled with anger, it is enough to simply confess it. However, if your anger has led you to violence, then offering a few additional details is important.[75]

CAN I JUST READ A LIST?

Yes. As we have already stated, it is perfectly acceptable to read a list. It is also okay for this list to be short. Confession does not need to take a lot of time.

IS THERE A DIFFERENCE BETWEEN CONFESSION AND SPIRITUAL ADVICE OR COUNSELING?

Yes. Pastoral counseling and confession are two different things. While we may seek counsel during confession, the confessional is for confessing our sins. You may need to make a separate appointment for spiritual counsel.

Do your best to keep your confession time for confessing sins, and save matters of discussion or direction for another appointment. Of course, depending on the parish and the priest, a time for confession and spiritual counsel can be combined. One last note: If the time offered for confessions is open to anyone who drops in

---

75   Offering a confession without preparing is okay as well. But as a general rule, preparing a confession is beneficial.

and you were not given a specific appointment time, remember that others may be waiting to confess after you. This may limit the amount of time available to speak with the priest.

CAN A PRIEST SHARE WHAT I TELL THEM?

The simple answer is no. In fact, the penalty for a priest violating the confessional is defrocking. This means a priest who shares what you tell him will be removed from serving as a priest by the Church. However, people sometimes mistake the preaching or advice a priest gives to his community for the sharing of what they told him in the confessional. This is probably not the case. Remember that most people's sins are the same, and general teaching from the pulpit is not personal—although it can feel that way.

HOW LONG DOES CONFESSION TAKE?

It varies. Nevertheless, your confession can be brief. Even life confessions, in which someone offers a confession of their entire life, can be done in less than ten minutes. People often tell me that they can't imagine how a confession can take such a short amount of time. But I can tell you that my own sins are many, and my confessions are short.

It is also helpful to understand that keeping our confessions short can guard against a type of pride and a misguided use of confession. Of course, if your confession takes longer, and if the priest has time for you, it is not wrong to take more time confessing.

WHAT TYPE OF MINDSET SHOULD I
HAVE WHEN I CONFESS?

To approach confession from a certain kind of fear is beneficial. Earlier I wrote against fear as an appropriate reason for confessing, and I stand by that comment. Yet having the right type of fear is helpful—a fear that recognizes the Lord's holiness and the authority He has over the living and the dead. This is a holy fear that realizes both God's sovereignty and the coming of Judgment Day.[76]

WILL I NOTICE SINS IN CONFESSION THAT I FAILED TO WRITE DOWN?

Yes, this often happens. Simply offer up these sins that come to mind during your confession.

WILL I NOTICE MY SINS TO A GREATER EXTENT OVER TIME?

Yes. The more we confess, the more we will notice our sins. As we grow toward Christ, we do not feel a greater sense of our holiness but the opposite. Yet in this frame of mind we do not despair or become despondent. Instead, we see with increasing clarity what is disfigured in our lives and what needs to be addressed. At the same time, we trust increasingly in God's mercy and love.

HOW MUCH DETAIL SHOULD I GIVE?

A few additional words on this subject are warranted. We can often feel the need to provide specifics regarding our sins, but in most instances this is not necessary. For example, certain sins often plague us, and as a result, confessing something like "I am often overcome with lust" is sufficient. On the other hand, we may

---

76 To fear judgment is not perfect, but it is a path toward salvation. A second motivation for confession is to pursue the reward of eternal life. This too is imperfect. The pursuit of what is good and true out of love for God and for His truth is the truest form of a Christian life.

find that certain sins, like lust, have led us to sin in other ways. This too should be confessed. Like a splinter, we want to remove all the sin and not leave something embedded in our soul that might fester.

WHAT SHOULD I NOT CONFESS?

This one is easy: The only thing we do not confess is the sins of another. This is important. If you want to ensure that your confession is appropriate, then you must do your best to avoid bringing up the sins of others. This includes blaming others for your own mistakes. Do your best to take responsibility for your sins, and leave it at that.

WHAT IF I DON'T HAVE MUCH TO SAY OR CAN'T THINK OF SINS TO CONFESS?

Forcing yourself to come up with sins is not the point. If you are not ready for confession or if you can't think of anything you'd like to confess, then take a step back and give yourself some time to pray and reflect.

DO I NEED TO FEEL BAD ABOUT MYSELF AND THE SINS I HAVE COMMITTED?

Keep in mind that "feeling" bad isn't necessary, and self-hatred is itself a sin. On the other hand, resolving to change your ways is a necessary part of confession. The feelings of contrition and sorrow over the harm you have caused yourself and others are also necessary. A priest is not supposed to offer the prayer of forgiveness if someone indicates that they do not intend on changing and that they don't believe the sin they have committed is wrong or harmful.

WHAT IF MY EXPERIENCE OF
CONFESSION IS NOT POSITIVE?

Unfortunately, the process of confession can go awry. This can happen in any number of ways. Years ago, a young woman who was entering the Church reached out to me to share her experience. After months of attending her local parish, she decided that she wanted to become a Christian. Repeatedly she approached the priest of the parish to tell of her desire to be baptized. Sadly, the priest was not responsive or helpful.

Eventually, he did tell the young woman that he'd set up a time for her to confess and be baptized. At this point, the young woman asked for resources to help her prepare, but none were given. Undeterred, she did what she could and showed up for confession. The priest met her and asked her to give her confession.

"Father," she said, "my desire to enter the Church has not left me, but I must admit I am disappointed by the fact that I have not received proper instruction or guidance. I am not even sure how or what confession is. For that matter, I don't even think I know what a sin is."

At this point the priest looked at her and said, "Well, you are wearing makeup, and that is a sin. You can start your confession with that." The young woman at that moment decided that perhaps she had made a grave mistake and that entering the Church was the wrong decision.

I was sad to hear what had occurred. I must admit that this story is one of the reasons I decided to write on this spiritual tool of the Church. While many people have positive experiences in their interactions with their local parish and its priest, this is not always the case. Priests bear such an important responsibility to provide good care and instruction. We must take this responsibility seriously. Of course, no priest is perfect, and I am sure that other factors came into play between this young woman and her local priest. I know that I too have not always done what I should and that I have wounded people unintentionally.

Nonetheless, sometimes things do not go well. We may have tried confessing our sins and found the experience to be hurtful and even damaging. In such an instance, what are we to do?[77] One thing we can do is ask others within the Church for a recommendation of a priest. We can also call the local bishop and ask him to recommend a priest to speak to. We can take our time and move cautiously at first, testing the waters. We can listen to our conscience and follow good common sense. Most importantly, we should not give up. We can pray and beseech God to direct us toward finding someone to confess to and from whom we can receive proper instruction and guidance.

WHAT IF I AM NOT ORTHODOX? CAN I STILL COME TO GIVE MY CONFESSION?

If you are not Orthodox, if you are inquiring into the Faith, or if you are a catechumen, the Sacrament of Confession is not available to you until you enter the Church through baptism and/or chrismation. At the same time, there is nothing that precludes you from confessing to God and, for that matter, to a priest. Many times people who are not Orthodox Christians have come to me to talk about or to confess their sins. I can't wear my vestments or offer the prayer of forgiveness as I would for someone who is a member of the Church, but I can as a representative of

---

77 As I stated earlier, any type of abuse within the confessional is unacceptable and cannot be tolerated. If you feel that you experienced abuse while giving your confession, you should speak to your bishop. You can also speak with a trusted friend or local priest.

Christ sit with them and listen to their confession as well as pray and offer counsel.

WHAT IF I DON'T FEEL FORGIVEN AFTER MY CONFESSION?

This is not uncommon. The thing we must be on the lookout for is whether or not we have accepted God's forgiveness. Often people feel that God can't forgive them. Here they must be reminded that nothing can stand in the way of God's love for us. It may help to remember what St. Paul wrote on this:

> What then shall we say to these things? If God *is* for us, who *can be* against us? He who did not spare His own Son, but delivered Him up for us all, how shall He not with Him also freely give us all things? Who shall bring a charge against God's elect? *It is* God who justifies. Who *is* he who condemns? *It is* Christ who died, and furthermore is also risen, who is even at the right hand of God, who also makes intercession for us. Who shall separate us from the love of Christ? *Shall* tribulation, or distress, or persecution, or famine, or nakedness, or peril, or sword? As it is written:
> "For your sake we are killed all day long;
> We are accounted as sheep for the slaughter."
> Yet in all these things we are more than conquerors through Him who loved us. For I am persuaded that neither death nor life, nor angels nor principalities nor powers, nor things present nor things to come, nor height nor depth, nor any other created thing, shall be able to separate us from the love of God which is in Christ Jesus our Lord. (Rom. 8:31–39)

There can exist in us a type of spiritual pride connected with our refusal to accept God's forgiveness. Years ago, I was struggling with a terrible sin I had committed. The problem was not that I didn't feel remorse or that I lacked a conviction to change my ways. My problem was I could not forgive myself for what I had done. During a powerful confession on the night before my ordination to the diaconate, I returned to this challenge I had with forgiving myself. In response my father confessor said to me, "Evan, well, it may be time for you to stop being a Christian."

"What?" I said. "How can you say this to me?"

He answered, "Look, God has forgiven you, but you have refused to forgive yourself. It sounds to me like your spiritual pride has gotten the best of you. For you to believe that your judgment is better than His means you think you are above God—better than God."

He was right. I needed to humble myself and accept that if God had forgiven me, then I needed to forgive myself.

WHAT IF I DECIDE TO KEEP CERTAIN SINS HIDDEN, OR I LACK A SENSE OF SORROW OR REMORSE OVER MY SIN?

The decision to keep a sin unconfessed typically has to do with embarrassment and a measure of unhealthy shame. I have rarely met someone who does not know the difference between right and wrong. The problem arises when it comes to doing what is right because it is uncomfortable or causes pain. We must, however, find the courage to confess our sin and to stand before God honestly and without excuse or false pride. Of course, a priest should not pry or "investigate" us during confession. He must respect our free will.

I once heard a piece of advice from an older priest related to confessing such sins. He told me that a spiritual child once asked him where they should begin their confession. The priest answered, "Start with the sin you least wish to share and are most ashamed of. After that, the rest of your confession will be painless and easy."

In terms of our feelings, once again, a correct response to sin is remorse and a sense that what we have done is harmful to ourselves and others.

SHOULD I CONFESS MY SINS TO DIFFERENT PRIESTS TO PROTECT MY IDENTITY?

No. I mentioned in the beginning of this chapter that anonymity is not a highly prized hallmark of the Church when it comes to confession. Think of it this way: Is it a good idea to ask someone who doesn't know you for advice about your life? The answer is obvious—it is not. In confession, it is better if the priest knows you and is familiar with your life and your struggles. This will give him insight regarding how to direct you. Additionally, our desire to remain anonymous is probably connected to unhealthy shame. We don't want someone to know our sin and to think badly of us, and, like Adam and Eve in the Garden, this type of shame leads us to hide our brokenness. Remember, what remains hidden remains unhealed.

HOW OFTEN SHOULD I GO TO CONFESSION?

The answer to this question depends a lot on several factors. Your father confessor may direct you to confess regularly. In some jurisdictions and parishes, parishioners participate in confession weekly. In other places, confession occurs less frequently. It can also vary based on what is going on in someone's life. There are times where more frequent confession is necessary. In my own parish, I counsel people to come to confession around four times a year. This number can go up or down, but the idea of four confessions per year matches up with the four great fasts of the Church: Great Lent (late winter and early spring), the Apostles' fast (typically in June), the Dormition fast (August 1–15), and the Nativity fast (November 15 through December 24).

HOW DO I HELP A CHILD OR FAMILY MEMBER PREPARE FOR CONFESSION?

The obvious answer is to go to confession yourself. Once I had a scheduled appointment with a couple in my parish. After praying, I asked which of them would like to go first for confession. The wife said, "I'll go first, and when I am done, I can give you his confession as well." Of course, confessing for someone else is not an acceptable spiritual practice in the Church. As we have already noted, it is not beneficial to look at the sins of others and judge them.

However, there are times when it is necessary to help a child, friend, or family member prepare for confession.[78] It can also be a good practice to seek the help of someone else when preparing. Sometimes they can aid us when it comes to seeing our sins.

Nevertheless, I can tell you from experience that it is not helpful to make an appointment for someone without their consent and participation. We don't "make" people go to confession, and when we do, the results are not good. Nor should we schedule a confession for a child and leave them alone in their preparation.

---

78 Helping a child prepare for confession is important. We should pray with them and assist them as they write out a list of sins they wish to confess. We may have to explain to them what confession is, what will happen, and why we confess our sins to a priest. If a child is nonverbal or cannot read but wishes to confess, we can use a preparation guide with pictures to help children identify what they wish to confess. Some helpful resources are available from the Raising Lazarus Project. You can find their website online and search for "confession tool" and other booklets for children.

DOES THE CHURCH EVER REQUIRE
US TO GO TO CONFESSION?

As I just said, we can never force a confession out of someone, nor should we. Yet, there are situations in which the Church encourages us to confess. Some examples of suggested times for confession are:

- after a long absence from receiving the Eucharist
- after a long absence from regular church attendance
- in preparation for our baptism and/or chrismation[79]
- before serving as a sponsor for a baptism or wedding
- when we are getting married
- before an operation, military deployment, extensive travel, or after an illness
- after committing a grave sin
- when we are stuck in a particular sin
- when leaving for college or before other major life events
- and, as mentioned above, during the great fasts.

DO I NEED TO GO TO CONFESSION EVERY TIME I SIN?

No. But confessing our sins every day before God—after examining our conscience—is very important and profitable. I think it makes sense to do this at the end of our day before sleep. We can also read one of the prayers from an Orthodox prayer book that asks for God's forgiveness. (I have included "A Daily Prayer for Forgiveness" on page 110.) Another good thing we can do is pray Psalm 50/51.[80]

---

79 Obviously this does not apply to infants. I have included a general prayer of forgiveness at the end of this chapter.

80 This particular psalm is beloved by the Church and appears in almost every service. In it the faithful are invited to reflect on the life of King David. During his lifetime David sinned greatly—he committed adultery and murder. To make matters worse, he hid this sin from others. In time,

SHOULD I CONFESS SINS I HAVE ALREADY
CONFESSED IN THE PAST?

As a general rule, no, you should not. Once you have confessed a particular sin, it is forgiven and forgotten by God (Ps. 102/103:12). However, we often commit the same sins time and time again. It would be nice if we could confess our lack of humility one time and never have to confess it again. However, pride has a way of sneaking back into our lives. In fact, the practice of offering a life confession more than once is not unheard of in the Church. That is not because the Church teaches that one's sins have not yet been forgiven but, rather, because we may find that the process of reviewing our lives periodically helps us move closer to Jesus and deeper in our repentance.

SHOULD I KEEP CONFESSING THE SAME SIN?

Often we keep repeating the same sins.[81] Time and again people come to me for confession and start by saying, "Father, I feel like the list of sins I have prepared is the same as the previous time." While this may feel true, it often is not. We make progress and we regress, but our

---

his sin was uncovered, and David repented. Part of his repentance is the psalm he wrote, Psalm 50 (Psalm 51 in Protestant Bibles). It is an almost perfect prayer for those who wish to repent.

81 When we find that the same sin keeps showing up in our lives, it is possible that our will has been seriously disfigured. Earlier we talked about the importance of our will and its liberation. When we sin, we harm this important aspect of our personhood. Repeating a sin again and again over time can impact our ability to avoid the sin. This is apparent in the lives of people who are addicted to alcohol, but it is also true for those of us addicted to our phones, anger, lust, or food. At no point would we say our free will is totally impaired or overridden by sin; instead, we recognize that we have become habituated, and to a degree our free will is being hijacked or bypassed. This does not remove our responsibility. This is an extremely dangerous state, and without serious spiritual care and repentance we may find ourselves trapped in a sin that will lead to our separation from God and others.

sins rarely stay exactly the same. The truth is that our spiritual lives move through different periods of growth, stagnation, and decline. In each stage, we can learn something. A habitual sin is difficult to heal and hard to overcome. Yet one thing is certain: If a sin that has gotten ahold of us is left unconfessed and unattended, it gets worse.

When my eldest daughter was little, I used to let her play in our backyard unattended as I watched from the kitchen window. Our yard had a split-rail fence that led to an open space, and she could easily crawl under it. Naturally, I repeatedly told her that she was not allowed to go near the fence but could play within the yard.

One day she decided to test the boundaries she had been given. From the kitchen window, I watched as she slowly walked closer and closer to the fence. Every few steps she would look back toward the house to see if I was watching her. Eventually she reached the fence and placed her hands on the top rail. At this point, I opened the sliding door and called her name. Immediately she pulled her hands off the fence, but as she did, she got a splinter.

When I asked her to come to me, she was reluctant; she even hid her hand. It was as if the Fall were being reenacted before my very eyes. Instead of coming forward and showing me the splinter (wound or sin) that had resulted from her disobedience, she hid it from me. I had to go pick her up and bring her to the house—this is similar to how the father in the story of the Prodigal Son responded to his son's sins.

As she sat in my lap, I tried several times to get her to show me her hand. She would not, and she began to cry. Even though she had never gotten a splinter before, her first response was to hide and keep me from seeing it! Eventually, I had to plead with her to open her hand and show me what had happened. Of course, she wouldn't listen to reason, and I had a very hard time explaining to her that if we left the splinter in, it would probably get infected.

Once I began the process of removing the splinter, her cries and tears increased to a fever pitch. However, once I removed the splinter and applied a Mickey Mouse bandage, a popsicle finally calmed her down. At that point, I explained to her how important it was for her to be honest with me and tell me she had a splinter—that her daddy was here to help.

This story illustrates what happens in confession. We return again and again with the same splinters, and one by one, with the help of our spiritual father, we remove them. Certainly, we hope that eventually we will learn to avoid violating the boundaries of what is good and safe for us. At the same time, during this process of boundary breaking, we don't wait for our disobedience to stop before confessing.

SHOULD I MAKE A PLAN AFTER CONFESSION ON HOW TO OVERCOME MY SINS?

Yes. This was discussed earlier. (See the section beginning on page 72.)

WHEN CAN I GO FOR CONFESSION?

Every priest and parish will handle this question differently. Some parishes have set times for confession; others require you to set up an appointment. It just depends, so check with your local priest or parish.

Resources

A Daily Prayer for Forgiveness Before Sleep

LORD, OUR GOD, BY YOUR goodness and mercy forgive all the sins I have committed this day in thought, word, and deed. [Specify your sins to God and repent of them.] Grant me peaceful and undisturbed sleep, and deliver me from all temptations and attacks of the evil one. Raise me up again in the morning that I may glorify You. For You are blessed, together with Your Son and Your Holy Spirit, now and always and unto the ages of ages. Amen.

The Prayers of the Priest over One Who Has Confessed[82]

MY SPIRITUAL CHILD, WHO HAVE made your confession to my humble person: I, a humble sinner, have no power to forgive sins on earth; only God can do that; but, trusting in the divinely spoken words that were addressed to the Apostles after the Resurrection of our Lord Jesus Christ, which said, "If you pronounce forgiven the sins of any, they are forgiven them; and if you pronounce unforgiven the sins of any, they remain unforgiven," we are bold to say: Whatever you have related to my humble and lowly person, and whatever you have failed to say either from ignorance or from forgetfulness, whatever it may be, may God forgive you in this present age and in the age to come.

[The priest now asks the penitent to kneel and places his epitrachelion (stole) and his hand over their head, reciting the prayer of absolution.]

May God who, through Nathan the Prophet forgave David when he confessed his sins, and Peter, when he wept bitterly for his denial; and the harlot who shed tears upon his feet; and the Publican; and the Prodigal; may this same God forgive you, through me a sinner, everything, both in this present age and in the age to come, and may he make you stand uncondemned before his dread Judgment Seat. As for the sins that you have confessed, have no further

---

82   *Priest's Service Book*, 149–51.

anxiety about them; go in peace. The grace of the Holy Spirit, through my insignificance, has loosened and forgiven. Through the prayers of our holy Fathers, Lord Jesus Christ, our God, have mercy on us and save us. Amen.

A Preparation for Confession by St. John of Kronstadt[83]

I, A SINFUL SOUL, CONFESS to our Lord God and Savior Jesus Christ, all of my evil acts which I have done, said or thought from baptism even unto this present day.

I have not kept the vows of my baptism, but have made myself unwanted before the face of God.

I have sinned before the Lord by lack of faith and by doubts concerning the Orthodox Faith and the Holy Church; by ungratefulness for all of God's great and unceasing gifts; His long-suffering and His providence for me, a sinner; by lack of love for the Lord, as well as fear, through not fulfilling the Holy Commandments of God and the canons and rules of the Church.

I have not preserved a love for God and for my neighbor nor have I made enough efforts, because of laziness and lack of care, to learn the Commandments of God and the precepts of the Holy Fathers.

I have sinned: by not praying in the morning and in the evening and in the course of the day; by not attending the services or by coming to Church only half-heartedly, lazily and carelessly; by conversing during the services, by not paying attention, letting my mind wander and by departure from the Church before the dismissal and blessing.

I have sinned by judging members of the clergy.

---

83 St. John of Kronstadt, "A Preparation for Confession," *Saint Nicholas Russian Orthodox Church,* accessed April 22, 2025, https://www.orthodox.net /confess/confmed.html.

I have sinned by not respecting the Feasts, breaking the Fasts, and by immoderation in food and drink.

I have sinned by self-importance, disobedience, willfulness, self-righteousness, and the seeking of approval and praise.

I have sinned by unbelief, lack of faith, doubts, despair, despondency, abusive thoughts, blasphemy and swearing.

I have sinned by pride, a high opinion of my self, narcissism, vanity, conceit, envy, love of praise, love of honors, and by putting on airs.

I have sinned: by judging, malicious gossip, anger, remembering of offenses done to me, hatred and returning evil for evil; by slander, reproaches, lies, slyness, deception and hypocrisy; by prejudices, arguments, stubbornness, and an unwillingness to give way to my neighbor; by gloating, spitefulness, taunting, insults and mocking; by gossip, by speaking too much and by empty speech.

I have sinned by unnecessary and excessive laughter, by reviling and dwelling upon my previous sins, by arrogant behavior, insolence and lack of respect.

I have sinned by not keeping my physical and spiritual passions in check, by my enjoyment of impure thoughts, licentiousness and unchastity in thoughts, words and deeds.

I have sinned by lack of endurance towards my illnesses and sorrows, a devotion to the comforts of life and by being too attached to my parents, children, relatives and friends.

I have sinned by hardening my heart, having a weak will and by not forcing myself to do good.

I have sinned by miserliness, a love of money, the acquisition of unnecessary things and immoderate attachment to things.

I have sinned by self-justification, a disregard for the admonitions of my conscience and failing to confess my sins through negligence or false pride.

I have sinned many times by my Confession: belittling, justifying and keeping silent about sins.

I have sinned against the Most-holy and Life-creating Mysteries of the Body and Blood of our Lord by coming to Holy Communion without humility or the fear of God.

I have sinned in deed, word and thought, knowingly and unknowingly, willingly and unwillingly, thoughtfully and thoughtlessly, and it is impossible to enumerate all of my sins because of their multitude. But I truly repent of these and all others not mentioned by me because of my forgetfulness and I ask that they be forgiven through the abundance of the Mercy of God.

"If we say that we have no sin, we deceive ourselves, and the truth is not in us. If we confess our sins, He is faithful and just to forgive us our sins and to cleanse us from all unrighteousness." (1 John 1:8–9)

CHAPTER THREE

Theology of Time

A S A YOUNG BOY, I fell in love with watches. I can remember one of my earliest timepieces: a blue-banded, white-faced Donald Duck watch. Believe it or not, I still have this watch, and it still keeps good time.

I can also recall my struggle with time. It started early in my life. I was a nervous and anxious child. Events like Christmas, summer break, or the upcoming visit of a cherished relative would result in a sleepless night or a carefully crafted paper calendar countdown that I would dutifully update at the close of each day.

In my adult life, my relationship with time has continued to cause all manner of struggles and also great joy. Meeting my wife, Stacy, is just one example of this. I remember fondly our first encounter. It is still fresh in my mind, even though nearly three decades have passed. There we stood talking when we first met, and although the ballroom was filled with hundreds of other people, they all slipped out of consciousness and time. As the popular phrase goes, time stood still. As late as it was, nearing midnight, we stood talking and talking and talking until the ballroom was empty and the clean-up crew began its work.

Conversely, my trip back to Colorado and a trip she took to Washington meant my experience of time as it related to her was altered. Now, instead of being in her presence, I was separated from her. Time seemed to pass in a painfully slow march between letters (yes, we met in that bygone era when people wrote letters to one another), phone calls, and visits. These gaps were hard to bear, and I felt like a small child again, counting down the days.

Like me, you have probably struggled with the passage of time. I'm sure you have looked for ways to escape the moments you are in, used your time unwisely, been bored, thought of time as something to kill, and generally looked for ways to disconnect from it. When I was younger, I spent many summer days and nights at my father's diner staring at a clock, wishing the minute hand would move faster. My twelve-hour shifts as a busboy seemed to move in slow motion. I quickly realized that living "in time" was hard and that my relationship to time was unhealthy.

Learning that time can be altered through our relationship with Jesus Christ changes things—at least, it did for me. I came to learn that time is one of the great spiritual tools of the Church, and I think you will find that the Orthodox theology of time will transform your life.

Kairos *and* Chronos

I HAVE LEARNED SO MUCH by counseling others. Through the years I have been privileged to sit with hundreds, if not thousands, of people—some of them teenagers, others middle aged, and some in their final days. It doesn't take long to recognize that the spiritual challenges each person faces are complex. Unfortunately, no matter someone's age, they probably haven't connected the difficulties they are going through with an unhealthy or absent theology of time. Most of us haven't thought about how we live in time or, said differently, where we are *in it*. As a result, people are surprised to find out just how much positive change can occur when they begin to see the Christian understanding of time and how to apply it in their lives.

For Christians, the first thing we need to try to understand is that time is something that can be sanctified. To understand what I mean, we have to step back and explain a bit of Christian theology. Unfortunately, the modern person has lost sight of the ancient Greeks' distinction between different kinds of time, conveyed through the words *chronos* and *kairos*. Having forgotten this distinction and failing to see how this directs our lives, we can quickly become disfigured.

Now, any discussion of time is challenging. This may not seem true at first. You see, I can say something like, "Yesterday I ate a doughnut for breakfast, but today I had a fruit smoothie, while tomorrow I am going to have a bagel," and you would easily understand what I mean. When talking in this way, I am talking about time as chronos, and you can probably guess the meaning of this ancient Greek word, as it looks a lot like the word *chronology*. Chronos is a way of expressing our understanding or experience of time as it marches forward in seconds, minutes, hours, days, and years. It is this version of time that rules over our lives, especially in the modern world. When we live in chronos, we observe day and night, summer and fall, birthdays and anniversaries. Chronos has a lost past, a fleeting present, and an unrealized future. When we experience chronos, time can be segmented and divided, and our experience of life can then be attributed to something that happened to us, is happening now, or will happen one day. Of course, we can never recover or retrieve the past, the moment that has just passed, or the moments ahead.

What we need to understand is that this is not true for God. Rather, for God WHO IS, the realities of chronos do not exist as they do for us.[84] We can say then that God does not experience time as past, present, and future; instead, time for God is never segmented or divided. Nonetheless, for every human being, as well as creation itself, life is experienced primarily as chronos.

The second term for time used by the ancient Greeks is *kairos*. This concept of time is a bit trickier to understand. It conveys something more like being in the opportune time, the appointed time, or the fitting time. To comprehend what I mean, imagine asking someone the question, "Did you have a good time at Christmas?" You would not be waiting to hear an answer that told you how many hours and minutes someone spent with their family! Your intent would be to understand more about the *quality of time spent* rather than its *quantity*.

Experiencing Time in a New Way

INTRODUCING A SECOND TERM FOR how we conceptualize time can be confusing. However, as we consider the concept of kairos, we recognize that this is but another word we can use to help us express our experience of time *not* as chronos. As I mentioned above, when I met my future wife, Stacy, for the first time, we talked late into the night. Honestly, we both lost track of time, and the hours passed by unnoticed. Chronology slipped away, and for us the time we spent talking could better be described as kairos, not chronos.

Kairos thus describes how we think of God's time, and it is related to the example I just gave. Interestingly, this word appears something like eighty-six times in the New Testament. Here we must introduce another aspect of our Christian understanding—namely,

---

84 WHO IS is one of the ways God identifies Himself: "I AM WHO I AM" (Ex. 3:14).

the fact that kairos can intersect with chronos, and when this happens, we experience time in a new way.

To illustrate what I mean, let's look at the opening chapter from the Gospel of Mark. We read in verses 14 and 15, "Now after John was put in prison, Jesus came to Galilee, preaching the gospel of the kingdom of God, and saying, 'The time is fulfilled, and the kingdom of God is at hand. Repent, and believe in the gospel.'"[85] We should note that the word translated here as "time" in verse 15 is *kairos*, not *chronos*.

As we consider this passage, we realize that St. Mark has offered us details about the start of Jesus' ministry: He has given us a chronology. This is why he tells us that after St. John the Forerunner and Baptist of our Lord was imprisoned, Jesus arrived in Galilee to begin His work. In chronological time, the events occur in succession: John's imprisonment, Jesus' arrival, the beginning of Jesus' work. Yet while the start of Jesus' ministry occurs on a specific day and at a specific hour, it is not confined to chronos alone. Rather, kairos has broken into chronos, and this is what the passage is telling us. To put it another way, the use of this word indicates that God is now acting in chronological time. The events being described to us in the Gospel are not happening apart from Him. This means that as the eternal touches ordinary time, time is not only changed but fulfilled.

At this point in our discussion, it might help to point out that most of us live life in a two-dimensional way. This means we don't consider that each so-called mundane moment of chronos can be connected with something outside of our chronologically bound experience of life. Living in this two-dimensional way means that

---

85   I think it is amazing to consider that in the first reference to time in the Gospel, the word used is *kairos*. This word choice is important, as the gospel of Christ is not presented to us in mere chronological terms.

time as kairos may not factor into our lives at all. Yet the experience of Christians is that kairos can and does intersect with time, with our lives, and this changes everything. When this happens, we begin to live in a three-dimensional way. It is like the transition in the movie *The Wizard of Oz*, when the director switches from black and white to color for the first time. In doing this he shows that life can and does operate at a deeper and multidimensional way.

Likewise, in these moments when chronos and kairos intersect, we realize God is present, and His Presence fundamentally alters our experience of life and, as we shall see, its outcome. This means washing the dishes, something we would typically describe as mundane, becomes something more, and so does helping a child learn to read, a task we would typically consider to be more profound. We can go further and say that these moments of life not only are experienced differently but also become sanctified. They become moments that carry within them the transforming power of God's Presence and moments that carry the power to transform our lives.

Opening—or Reopening—Ourselves to God's Presence

THIS NEW PERSPECTIVE OFFERS US a different way of understanding time: specifically, the belief that when kairos inserts itself into chronos, as it did when Jesus began preaching, we are not bound to experience life as an expression of chronology alone. This intersection of the infinite Lord with chronological life brings a fulfillment—a glimpse of eternity, a life filled with the Presence of God—to chronos. Conversely, when we continue to live "in time" without kairos, then time remains unredeemed and even corrosive.

This statement may seem at first drastic or even a bit of a stretch. Yet this is exactly the case. Some have heard me use the term "functional atheism." What I mean is that Christians who profess faith in God not only should express their belief in a sense of time that is transformed and redeemed by God, but should also live as if this truth impacts and directs their lives. Too often even Christians go about life like the Christians whom St. James criticized in his epistle:

> Come now, you who say, "Today or tomorrow we will go to such and such a city, spend a year there, buy and sell, and make a profit"; whereas you do not know what *will happen* tomorrow. For what *is* your life? It is even a vapor that appears for a little time and then vanishes away. Instead you *ought* to say, "If the Lord wills, we shall live and do this or that." (James 4:13–15)

These Christians failed to recognize the ever-present and life-sustaining Presence of God. They were living as if God were not real or active in their lives.

When we live in time without kairos, we come to experience an absence of God's Presence and live like those criticized by St. James. The truth is that God does have something to do with every moment, but He does not force Himself upon us. His Presence is like the hard-to-believe truth that the sun shines every day in Seattle. Having lived there, I can attest to the feeling that those monotonous, cloudy days will never end. Residents come to believe that the sun itself has disappeared.

Likewise, we can come to believe that God, who is not seen or felt, does not exist. Yet, when we open (or reopen) ourselves to the truth of His continual appearance in chronos via kairos, the experience is like an airplane breaking through the clouds. As it rises through them, the sun becomes apparent, and light streams into the cabin.

I remember the first flight I took out of Seattle after living there for several months without experiencing a sunny day. The climb out of Sea-Tac Airport was a welcome reminder to me in my window seat that the sun shines every day. In that moment I re-realized that the sun had been there all along, and so is God. When moments become enlivened by God, life is no longer mundane, and the disfiguring experience of chronos departs. In this state, we no longer look for ways to waste our time, to avoid its so-called drudgery, or even to fill our time with distraction to escape the boredom or pain of living solely in chronology. Instead, time ceases to be our enemy, and our attempt to live in chronos while seeking its fulfillment in life becomes joy. Moreover, our experience of time because of the joy of God's Presence takes on an eternal meaning and loses its painful qualities. In this fulfilled mode of existence, we take up our true nature: beings built to live in the Kingdom of God and designed to behold the beauty and truth of God rather than creatures bound to the base pleasures of life. In this sanctified state, gone is the incessant desire to increasingly seek pleasure, power, and distraction—really, anything that distracts us—and in its place, we find peace and purpose.

This experience of time being altered by the eternal is not uncommon to people who experience the Divine Liturgy for the first time. They realize that the Liturgy operates somehow differently than mere chronological time. The opposite is also true; many find the Liturgy laborious, long—even tedious. They wonder why so many phrases and prayers seem to repeat themselves. For them, chronos has a deep hold, and sitting through a long worship service is just another painful experience of time. Yet in the lives of the saints and those who have matured spiritually, their experience of the Liturgy is heavenly. They feel the service is a time unlike any other, and time as it is normally experienced in chronos slips away.

We note both in Holy Scripture and in our lives that the conver-
gence of kairos with chronos can be consequential, as when Jesus
began preaching; it can be miraculous, as when He healed the
blind man (John 9); and it can be mundane, as when we wash the
dishes or work a twelve-hour shift as a busboy. Nonetheless, in each
moment of our lives the possibility exists that chronos can be fulfilled and sanctified by living in the kairos of God—by our living
with an awareness of His Presence, His actions.

Perhaps the best way to understand this is through the experience of companionship. When we fall in love with someone, we
begin the lifelong journey of connecting our lives to theirs. Soon
any decision or action becomes combined with the thought "What
does my beloved want or desire?" Similarly, when we live with
God—when kairos has fulfilled chronos—then all that we think
and do is connected to Him. He is our constant companion.

I experienced this as a child when I came to understand the deep
connection that existed between my grandmother and my grandfather. There was the sense that they each lived with the other,
always, even when the other was not "in the room." I have experienced this in my own marriage. I can say that there aren't many
moments, big or small, when I don't first consider my beloved. She
too is a constant companion to my life.

Results of the Fall in Our Experience of Time

IT WOULD BE LOVELY TO live every moment of our lives at the intersection of kairos and chronos, but as anyone can tell you, this is
not what we experience. Instead, as a result of the Fall, we usually
find ourselves trapped in an experience of time as chronos. This, of
course, was not what God intended. Rather, in the Garden, Adam
and Eve experienced time differently than we do now. Before the

Fall, they walked in communion with God and each other. To envision this (we will discuss this to a greater extent later), we must simply understand that communion with God is an experience that can occur only in the present. Additionally, we must remind ourselves that sin at its most basic level is anything that breaks our communion with God and one another. After the Fall, our relationship with the Lord and with each other became tenuous. We are connected often by the thinnest of strings, and the time we spend with one another becomes fragmented. We may find that deep connections between ourselves and others, the very thing we were created for, become difficult and hard to sustain.

To understand more fully this break between kairos and chronos in the Fall, we need to examine some of the consequences. What we find is that the loss of an integrated framework for time results in a fractured, fragmented, and disfigured existence. Simply put, our experience of life becomes separated from the Presence of God and the presence of others, and our experience of time as chronos stands alone and is no longer fulfilled by kairos. As we mentioned above, living in this way leads to a type of functional atheism. In this state, humankind finds itself disordered and lost. Not only does humanity find itself after the Fall trapped in time as chronos; we also cling to our chronology, thus losing sight of eternity.

I observed the consequences of this point of view when someone I knew received the terrible news that their cancer had returned. For them the news was tragic, as it would be, of course, for all of us. Yet this news carried with it a sense of hopelessness because their view of life had been bound to chronos. All that they valued and everything they hoped for was tied to this life.

The equation and meaning they had worked out when it came to time was simple: More time on earth was better than less time. This equation, coupled with the news that they would not live much longer, embittered them. They told me that they felt cheated, and that life and death itself were unfair. Making their diagnosis worse was the fact that they had never considered that life could be more than the accumulation of years—and, in their words, things. Their remaining days became increasingly painful not only in a physical sense but in an emotional, psychological, and spiritual sense. Bitterness became cynicism and an overriding desire to grasp at anything that might give them more time, no matter the quality.

Tragically, their last months were not filled with connection, conversation, and moments spent with loved ones. Rather than spend their remaining time with others, they spent their final days in waiting rooms, in desperate internet searches for cures, and in greater and greater isolation.

An alternative approach to our suffering and mortality is to recognize that time can be sanctified and life can be transformed. With this in mind, our goal is not simply more time, but time fulfilled—time that escapes the confines of the Fall, this world, and our disfigured ways. This happens when life is filled with God's Presence and the loving presence of others. This reality is the meaning of chronos fulfilled by kairos. It is not limited by our earth-bound attempts to prolong chronological time indefinitely.

A relative of mine once asked me what I thought of the idea that humanity through technology would eventually conquer death. His perspective was that this would render "my job" as a priest meaningless. I remember thinking how naïve and shortsighted his point of view was. Avoiding death doesn't solve our problems; conquering sin does. Ironically, the Gospel teaches us that Jesus Christ conquered both sin and death, and through faith in Him, so can we.

The Consequences of Unfulfilled Chronos

THE VIEW OF LIFE THAT values chronos alone has many tragic and unhealthy consequences. In the case of my acquaintance, it meant that they could not operate in a rightly ordered way with God, with others, and with the world. For my relative, it meant they would overlook the reality of sin, which is what really harms us. This fragmented existence and our experience of it cannot be overstated. I too have found myself disordered and lost when I've placed my hope in this life alone and in an experience of time dominated by chronos. In such a state, I have discovered that what God created as integrated and whole is shattered. More importantly, living in this broken state means holiness is no longer possible as we become increasingly bound to this life and its promises. It is in this mode of fractured time that we sin.[86]

One perspective of this shattered state comes to us in the Gospel of Luke. In the fifteenth chapter, which contains the well-known Parable of the Prodigal Son, we read about a young man who leaves his father's home, taking half of his father's goods and his full inheritance. He journeys into a far country, and "there [he] wasted his possessions with prodigal living" (Luke 15:13b). The Greek of the text here is worth noting: διεσκόρπισεν τὴν οὐσίαν αὐτοῦ (the-eh-score-pea-sen, teen, ousee-an, off-too). What we learn is that the younger son had dispersed, or scattered, his substance. The scholar Fr. Maximos Constas says,

> On one level this means that he squandered all his money, but the
> deeper meaning is the wealth of the soul, our spiritual inheritance,

---

86   As St. John warned, "Do not love the world or the things in the world. If anyone loves the world, the love of the Father is not in him. For all that *is* in the world—the lust of the flesh, the lust of the eyes, and the pride of life—is not of the Father but is of the world. And the world is passing away, and the lust of it; but he who does the will of God abides forever" (1 John 2:15–17).

since our "substance" is the spirit that God has placed within us, and in which, through Holy Baptism, He has planted His own grace, clothing us in "our original garment of glory" (cf. Lk. 15:22) and "sending forth His own Spirit into our hearts." (Gal. 4:6)[87]

When we separate ourselves from this grace, we lose our spiritual unity and become fragmented.[88] Fragmentation occurs on many levels. Each part of us suffers to some degree—our thoughts, our hearts, our minds, and our nous.[89] What is worrisome is that we ignore this shattering of time in the human person. Instead of seeking a reintegration of kairos with chronos, where the ever-present God breaks into our lives, we now seek its opposite and, like Adam and Eve, move away from Him.

Outside God's Presence

IN GENESIS WE READ ABOUT the Fall of humankind and, specifically, the exchange between God and Adam afterward:

And they heard the sound of the LORD God walking in the garden in the cool of the day, and Adam and his wife **hid themselves** [emphasis mine] from the **presence** [emphasis mine] of the LORD God among the trees of the garden.

Then the LORD God called to Adam and said to him, "Where *are* you?"

---

87   Fr. Maximos Constas, "'Πρόσεχε σεαυτῷ': Attentiveness and Digital Culture," paper presented at the International Conference on Digital Media and Orthodox Pastoral Care, Athens, May 7–9, 2015, https://www.academia.edu/12365160/.

88   Constas, "'Πρόσεχε σεαυτῷ,'" 5.

89   The "eye of the soul."

So he said, "I heard Your voice in the garden, and I was afraid because I was naked; and I hid myself." (Gen. 3:8–10)

When Adam and Eve sinned, they sinned outside the Presence of God. Moreover, while in this state of sin they remained outside God's Presence, and so they hid themselves. It is important to recognize that when God encounters Adam and Eve, He asks simply, "Adam, where are you?" This question is an attempt by God to "locate" Adam. Is it possible that God lost him? No. Rather, I think the meaning is deeper: Adam and Eve have through sin left God's *Presence*, and now He will need to bring them back into the *present* and thus His Presence.

To understand this better, consider the account of the life of Jesus in Holy Scripture. We note that the demons cannot exist in the Presence of Christ; whenever He is present, they must leave. In the eighth chapter of St. Matthew's Gospel, we read that when Christ encountered two demon-possessed men, the demons immediately cried out and asked if they could be cast into the nearby swine. Christ simply said "Go" (v. 32), and they did. But notice in that passage that Christ's *Presence* is what upset the demons; they could not be present with Him because they cannot exist in the same space of time where He is; demons cannot remain in His Presence.[90]

Our Struggle with Being Present

WE BELIEVE OUR LORD'S LIFE and ministry is restorative and healing and that by following His example we come to understand how

---

90   Jesus through His Presence alone is constantly pushing back and destroying the world of evil and sin. (Later we will note that this world is often labeled the world of fantasy by the Desert Fathers.) Truthfully, any spiritual progress we hope to make can occur only when we are grounded in Christ and thus in reality.

to live rightly with time. This allows us to become reintegrated and whole and, most importantly, makes it possible to live in the Presence of God and one another. Additionally, one of the points I will make in this section is essential to our understanding of living in time rightly: We must learn to live in the present moment as much as possible.

To help people understand what I am talking about, I often use this simple timeline:

•······ The Past (fantasy) ·····• ··· The Future (fantasy) ····•

Imagine that the dot on the far left is the day you were born and the dot on the far right is the day you will die. We of course do not know the date of our death, but for the purpose of this analogy, we don't need to—only that it is in the future. The dot in the middle is where you are right this moment.

Next, as you know, everything from the moment you were born until this very moment we call the past, while everything from right now until the day you die is the future. Of course, the moment you are in currently is the present. For the purposes of what we are saying, it is important to note that the saints of the Church label the past and the future as fantasy. Unlike our modern use of the word, this label is neither innocuous nor positive. For them, the world of fantasy is a spiritually dangerous "place." It is a world inhabited not by God but by the demons.

Returning to this timeline, ask yourself two questions:

1. Where am I in this timeline?
2. Where is God?

To the first question, most people answer, "Naturally I'm here, so I'm in the present." This is, sadly, a great lie we tell ourselves that leads us to ignore the fact that we spend the majority of our time allowing our minds to live in both the past and the future (the world of fantasy). We are each consumed, to a greater or lesser degree, with thoughts of what we *did* and what we are *going to do*—so much so that we ignore and become absent from the present, which is the moment we are living.[91]

The reality of our situation is this: We are soul sick. Thus, where we live within our thought lives is a mixture of the past and future, with only fleeting moments of being in the present.

Another way of saying this is that we live mostly in unfulfilled chronos, fragmented and apart from God and each other, and thus infrequently in kairos. We struggle mightily with being present. In fact, our thoughts and thus our actions are dominated not by what we are experiencing right now but by fantasies of the past and fantasies of the future. For example, our thoughts will alternate and skip between reminiscing about the good old days and considering the things of tomorrow. This is a perverted spiritual state, and we can become trapped in these fantasies, losing touch with the present and thus with reality.

Making matters worse is the truth that calling ourselves into the present moment is incredibly difficult, and our ability to do so is diminished with every passing moment we squander by living in this fractured and fragmented way.[92] All this inner fragmentation

---

91 This reality of ignoring the present is a consequence of a few things: first, the Fall of humankind in the Garden and being trapped in chronos; second, the increasing levels of distraction and fragmentation we discussed earlier; and third, our failure to live sacramentally, where our moments are taken up and fulfilled by the Presence of God—chronos fulfilled by kairos.

92 Every moment we spend seeking distraction can be dangerous. In fact, this pursuit, if unchecked, compounds, and over time we find it increasingly

has an increasingly negative and corrosive impact on our relationships with God and one another. Thankfully, being in the present
is a skill we can develop, but it requires that we work at it. This is
something we will talk about later in the chapter.

For now, to illustrate our struggle with being present, try answer-
ing the following three questions:

- What is the most important moment in your life?
- Who is the most important person in your life?
- What is the most important thing you have done?

The correct answers are:

- Now.
- The person in front of you.
- What you are doing right now.

To return to the earlier question "Where is God?," the most common response I receive is that God is "over the whole timeline; He is
everywhere." People usually express this by stating something like
the idea that God is "outside of time" or "above time."

While this sentiment is an honest one, it may not be helpful. Look
again at that timeline and, specifically, the middle point—the now.
This is where God is. He is found *right now*, not in the past or future.

In the letters of St. Paul we find evidence for this point of view.
The great apostle writes,

---

difficult to reverse and be present. In this disordered state, activities like
prayer, the remembrance of God, and the ability to attend to ourselves is
lost. In this state, what need do the demons have to persuade us toward
evil? Very little, because, like the Prodigal Son, after dispersing ourselves
through chasing every mental trinket, our inner self becomes tattered
beyond recognition.

We then, *as* workers together *with Him* also plead with *you* not to receive the grace of God in vain. For He says:

"In an acceptable time I have heard you,

And in the day of salvation I have helped you."

Behold, **now** [emphasis mine] *is* the accepted time; behold, **now** [again emphasis mine] *is* the day of salvation. (2 Cor. 6:1–2)

At this point, you probably have guessed that in both instances where the word *time* appears, the word St. Paul uses is *kairos*. Nevertheless, this passage, like many others, shows us where God is in time: now. We have been assured of His constant Presence in every moment of our lives. In fact, right before Jesus ascended into heaven, He reassured us, saying, "I am with you always, *even* to the end of the age" (Matt. 28:20).[93] For centuries these words of Christ have not only comforted Christians but reminded them that the Lord God is present in the here and now.

Of course, our failure to live in the present and recognize His Presence in the now gets us into trouble. God's time, as we have pointed out, is not confined to our sense of chronology. Instead, the fulfillment of chronos occurs as it intersects with kairos. When we notice this, we realize that God has broken into the mundane moments of our lives.

Fractured Time and Its Consequences

IMAGINE A YOUNG LADY WHO believes that every bit of her stress will be taken care of if she just obtains X. That could be a career, a

---

93 This particular quotation comes from a passage of Scripture known commonly as the Great Commission, in Matthew 28:18–20. The passage relates to the Lord's abiding Presence and how He will never depart from us. I wrote a book based on this passage, *Reclaiming the Great Commission: A Roadmap to Parish Health*, in which I explore these last words of Christ and their impact on outreach and evangelism.

house, a husband, kids, or any number of other things. She dreams of having a fairy-tale life and operates with the notion that if she can just get there, everything else will be fine.

The problem is that it won't be. Instead, as she marches forward in time thinking of her future fragmented from kairos, her experience of the present is splintered—just as it was in her past. Specifically, the person who focuses on things in the future, like this young woman has, will become riddled with anxiety. They will constantly worry about what is *out there* and, as a result, fail to engage in the present where God resides.

Now think of an older gentleman. He lives constantly in the past. "If I had just [fill in the blank], then things would be different!" This could be something like "I could have been a pro ball player" or "I could have gotten that promotion" or several other options that all lead to the same place—leading a life of regret that quickly turns into bitterness. This resentment then becomes outwardly directed anger that results in his failing to engage with the present where God resides—or to engage with others whom God has placed in his path.

Let's ask the second question, "Where is God?," again, but in a slightly different way: "Where in the timeline of our lives is Jesus?" Again, most of us are tempted to answer, "Everywhere." However, as we have already said, this answer can be misleading. Christ is of course Lord of all things, but He can be experienced only in the present, for the present is the only time that actually *is* for us. In this sense, we can say that **His Presence is *in* the present** and not in the past, which no longer exists, or in the future, which has not yet come to pass.[94]

---

94   Again, in the Church, the past and the future in this context are understood in a negative way; they are the realm of fantasy, and as such they are spiritually dangerous and disfiguring. When we spend our time there, we are accompanied not by God but by demons.

We cannot recover the past, and we cannot assume the future; the only time that matters is *now*. Of course, our past can greatly impact the present moment, and so can our plans for the future. But what we can do can be done only now, when chronos is altered and fulfilled by kairos. This is how the present can be transformed. In the Prophet Isaiah we read, "Look to Me, and be saved, All you ends of the earth! For I *am* God, and *there is* no other" (Is. 45:22). Developing the ability to return ourselves from our visits into our pasts and futures allows us to encounter God. By encountering God in the now, kairos fulfills chronos.

I AM

To illustrate this point further, let's turn our attention to another place in the Scriptures. In this passage we enter into Jesus' dialogue with His disciples right before His arrest. The Lord is comforting His followers, whose fears and worries are in many ways attached to their inability to stay present:

> "Let not your heart be troubled; you believe in God, believe also in Me. In My Father's house are many mansions; if *it were* not *so*, I would have told you. I go to prepare a place for you. And if I go and prepare a place for you, I will come again and receive you to Myself; that where **I am** [emphasis mine], *there* you may be also. And where I go you know, and the way you know."
>
> Thomas said to Him, "Lord, we do not know where You are going, and how can we know the way?"
>
> Jesus said to him, "**I am** [emphasis mine] the way, the truth, and the life." (John 14:1–6)

One of the keys to understanding this passage of Scripture is the following: Because our minds choose to live in the past or future and have forgotten to live in the present, we often live outside the Presence of Christ.[95] Thus it could be argued that to be *in His Presence*, we must be *in the present*. This is not easy, but when we face life's challenges, like the disciples we must remember that God's Presence can be found only *now*—in this present moment. This truth changes everything.

A beautiful passage from the Bible further illustrates this idea of God's Presence in the present moment. When God first utters His Name, or when He first shares His identity, He does so in this way:

> Then Moses said to God, "Indeed, *when* I come to the children of Israel and say to them, 'The God of your fathers has sent me to you,' and they say to me, 'What *is* His name?' what shall I say to them?"
> And God said to Moses, "I AM WHO I AM." (Ex. 3:13–14)[96]

Much of our modern culture has taken this as a declarative statement of power and nothing more—who God is—without recognizing that the words also relate to *when* God is.

Similarly, when Jesus is asked to identify Himself, He answers in the same way, as recorded multiple times in the Gospel of John: "I am the light of the world" (8:12); "I am the bread of life" (6:35); "I am the door" (10:9); "I am the good shepherd" (10:11 and 10:14); "I am

---

95 Of course, God is present everywhere; however, when we fail to live in the present, we fail to recognize this reality.

96 The Hebrew phrase *Ehyeh Asher Ehyeh* conveys the idea of God's self-existence and eternal nature. It is translated in various ways and can mean "I AM the Existing One." Those who have been inside an Orthodox Church may have noticed that a dome is often located in the middle of the church. Depicted in the dome is an icon called the Pantocrator (the Almighty). The icon depicts Jesus, Lord of heaven and earth, looking down and over His Church, His people, and creation. Often the words written around this circular icon are those found in Exodus 3:13–14.

the way, the truth, and the life" (14:6). *I Am* is a recurring theme for a reason.

I have become fond of this poem by Helen Mallicoat that reminds us of God's Presence in the present:

> I was regretting the past and fearing the future. Suddenly, my Lord was speaking: "My Name is I AM." He paused. I waited. He continued: "When you live in the past, with its mistakes and regrets, it is hard. I am not there. My name is not I WAS. When you live in the future, with its problems and fears, it is hard. I am not there. My name is not I WILL BE. But when you live in this moment, it is not hard. I am here. My Name is I AM."[97]

In another place, we read in Holy Scripture that "God is love" (1 John 4:8). Let me reemphasize that we learn not that God *was* love or that God *will be* love one day. Instead, we read that God *is* love. Such an understanding of love should lead us to the realization that the virtues exist only in the present. Another way of thinking about this is to ask yourself, "How can I be loving, merciful, humble, or generous in the past or the future?" The truth is, you cannot; you cannot be merciful in the future. It is not possible. We can only show mercy *right now*.

When I think about this, I often recall John, the disciple who laid his head on the breast of Jesus during His Last Supper with the twelve disciples—their last meal on earth together (John 13:23). This description is powerful. John placed his head and thus his ear on the bosom of Christ. Of course, St. John had heard and seen the teachings and miracles of Christ, but this act was

---

97   Helen Mallicoat, *Listen for the Lord: God's Messages of Love, Guidance and Inspiration* (Hallmark Cards, 1977).

transformative, and it cannot be overlooked. In this position, John heard Jesus' heartbeat.

I remember doing the same with my mom and my grandmother. That act and the tenderness of it brought me out of the disorientation of my past and future and put me right into the present and the presence of another. Saint John, having experienced this, was thus able to speak of love and imitate it. It is out of his experience of Christ's heart, Christ's love in the present, that he entered into the Lord's abiding Presence. "God is love, and he who abides in love abides in God, and God in him" (1 John 4:16).

Our Disordered Relationship with Time

WHAT CAN WE LEARN FROM the time we spend in the past or future? The cause of many of our spiritual illnesses is our disordered relationship with time. This is what we have been describing thus far. However, a look at the symptoms is beneficial; in meeting with people one on one, I start with the symptom and work backward to the cause.

THE PAST

WE CAN LOOK AT THE sicknesses of our soul through our disordered experience of time. For example, when we allow our hearts and thoughts to dwell in the past, we live with anger, bitterness, regret, cynicism, and depression, to name a few. I think it is helpful at this point to do a bit of soul searching of your own. Stop and think about your relationship with time and the past and how this has manifested itself in your life. I think you will find a few more examples of how your life has been upended, and not for the better, through living in the past (the realm of fantasy).

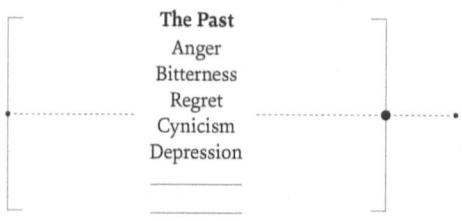

THE FUTURE

LIKEWISE, THE SICKNESSES OUR SOUL experiences from living in fantasies of the future are equally damaging. We should note that some of the sins we experience when we live in the future can also be attributed to the past and vice versa. A short list of some of the sins we experience when we live in the future includes ingratitude, discontent, worry, anxiety, impatience, and fear.

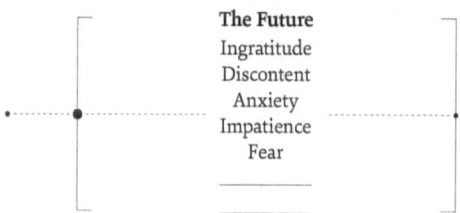

THE PROBLEM WITH FANTASY

UNFORTUNATELY, MENTALLY LIVING IN THE past or future means we are living in the world of fantasy. This is not a good thing. In the Church's understanding of time, the world of fantasy is the world of the demons. Saint Hesychios the priest explained,

> The demons always lead us into sin by means of deceitful fantasies. . . . The heart which is constantly guarded, and is not allowed to receive the forms, images and fantasies of the dark and

evil spirits, is conditioned by nature to give birth from within itself to thoughts filled with light. For just as coal engenders a flame, or a flame lights a candle, so will God, who from our baptism dwells in our heart, kindle our mind to contemplation when He finds it free from the winds of evil and protected by the guarding of the intellect.[98]

In this space of mental fantasy, the demons, who have no real substance, abide; it is the land of shadows, half-truths, and lies. While we rummage around in this fantasy land, we sin. It just might be that we cannot sin while in the present but only when we dwell in the past or future.[99] Saint Basil addresses the dangers of fantasy in his second preparation prayer before communion:

Therefore have compassion, O Lord, and do not make an example of me, a sinner, but deal with me according to Thy mercy; and let these Holy Things be for my healing and purification and enlightenment and protection and salvation and sanctification of body and soul, for the turning away of every fantasy and all evil practice and diabolical activity working subconsciously in my members.[100]

I love this prayer of St. Basil. His insight into where the demons attack is so helpful and true. They enter our lives when we spend time in fantasy.

---

98 St. Hesychios, "On Watchfulness and Holiness," in *The Philokalia*, trans. Kallistos Ware, G. E. H. Palmer, and Philip Sherrard, 5 vols. (Faber and Faber, 1979–2023), 1:118 and 182; 104 and 180.

99 In describing the Prodigal Son's descent into sin, the Blessed Theophylact writes, "Understand that when he sinned, he behaved as if he were not acting in the sight of God, that is, in the presence of God." Blessed Theophylact, *The Explanation of the Holy Gospel According to Luke*, trans. Fr. Christopher Stade, vol. 3 (Chrysostom Press, 2007), 199.

100 From the *Small Ieratikon*, Greek Orthodox Metropolis of Denver, 2008.

Certainly, one could argue that such an idea is preposterous. People sin all the time, and when they do so, they sin in the present. After all, none of us is able to time travel. You might ask, "How can you sin in the past or the future when they do not exist?" My point is not that one who sins does so in the actual past or the soon-to-be-realized future. Rather, a person sins in the fractured state that exists when they no longer maintain that precious connection between the One Who Is and the moment they live in, right now. In fact, the saints argue that the beginning of sin is the forgetting of God. To say this another way, when we are in the past or the future, rather than in the present, we metaphysically or spiritually detach from God's Presence. It is in this state that we sin. We become fragmented and fractured *in time*; we become disconnected from God and inhabit the world of fantasy. In this state, we find ourselves divorced from God and attached to demons. We wander and infrequently return from this space, and when we return, we are no better because of our sojourn in this half-life existence.

Through His Presence, Jesus in fact pushes back and destroys the world of fantasy. Numerous accounts in the Gospels describe Jesus' confrontation with evil and sin and thus with the world of fantasy. In each, He is victorious. One such example occurs in the Gospel of Matthew 16:21–23. Here the Disciple Peter rebukes Christ, who has shared with the Twelve that soon He must go to Jerusalem, where He will suffer, die, and rise from the dead. Peter attempts to direct the Lord away from His purpose and the divinely appointed intersection of kairos into chronos. Peter loses touch with the reality of Christ's Presence and His purpose in time, and this is why Jesus so forcefully redirects him.

Truthfully, any spiritual progress we hope to make can be done only when we are grounded in reality in the Presence of Christ. An imagination that considers what should be done (as in the case of

St. Peter) or reminisces over the spiritual accomplishments of the past (as often happens in my own mind) has hijacked us. This perverted state convinces us that our fantasies are reality. They waste our time and keep us from living in the present and thus in the Presence of Christ.

Seeking Distraction

ONE COULD ARGUE THAT WE have become indiscriminate and indifferent when it comes to our seeking distractions that lead to fragmentation. The twenty-first-century person lives in a world of distraction—some even enjoy this state. The rise of technologies and media compounds this soul-destroying state because they are designed specifically to disconnect us from the present and any attention we might pay to ourselves or the Presence of God.

We all know that these technologies have rapidly increased, and so has our addiction to distracted and fragmented living. This has further distanced us from living in fulfilled chronos. Many seek distraction and the dissociation from reality that it offers. We pursue this manner of living no matter how it corrodes our ability to encounter God and others.

Why do we seek distraction, and why do we struggle to stay present? An answer can be found in the following: All of us at one point or another experience the daily discomforts that come from living in an imperfect world. These experiences lead to our desire to avoid life's challenges, pain, and discomfort. Our solution is often to seek distraction.

Of course, there are a host of reasons for challenging and painful experiences. Yet, these hardships, whether large or small, are a part of life. In fact, Christ tells us that while in this life we will always experience tribulation and trials (John 16:33).

Sometimes the difficulties we face are minor, like waking up with a sore throat. Other times they are life-changing, like finding out that a close friend has betrayed us. Sometimes the pain we experience is self-inflicted, like when we tell a lie and it is discovered, resulting in the loss of another's trust. At other times, sorrow finds us, as in the unexpected and tragic loss of a loved one.

Jesus Came to Rescue and Restore Creation

IT IS UNIVERSALLY TRUE THAT a healthy human being does not enjoy pain; nor do they look for hardship and sorrow. Moreover, it is the teaching of Christianity that God did not create us for either. Creation was not meant to be a crucible of misery and an ongoing slog through trials and tribulations, ending in death. Rather, the story of creation shows life as Paradise (Gen. 2:15). It also describes our eternal condition in the same way. In other words, we were created by God to live without pain and discomfort.

In the memorial service of the Orthodox Church, a phrase in one of the prayers reminds us of this reality. In our prayer we say,

> O God of spirits and of all flesh, You trampled upon death and abolished the power of the devil, giving life to Your world. Give rest to the soul(s) of Your departed servant(s) (*Name*) in a place of light, in a place of green pasture, in a place of refreshment, from where pain, sorrow, and sighing have fled away. As a good and loving God, forgive every sin he (*she, they*) has (*have*) committed in word, deed, or thought, for there is no one who lives and does not sin. You alone are without sin. Your righteousness is an everlasting righteousness, and Your word is truth.[101]

---

101 *Priest's Service Book*, 207.

The Gospels tell us that this is why Jesus came: to rescue and restore creation from this disfigured state.[102] The Book of Revelation describes heaven this way: "And God will wipe away every tear from their eyes; there shall be no more death, nor sorrow, nor crying. There shall be no more pain, for the former things have passed away" (Rev. 21:4).

Transformation through Suffering

THE MANNER OF JESUS' RESCUE and the way of our restoration are at first glance problematic. What we come to find out is that Jesus' plan includes the very thing we wish to avoid—suffering. We learn that God's plan is not a plan that magically or miraculously delivers us from the sorrows of this world but instead uses them and transforms them. A passage from Holy Scripture describes this:

"Now My soul is troubled, and what shall I say? 'Father, save Me from this hour'? But for this purpose I came to this hour. Father, glorify Your name."

Then a voice came from heaven, *saying*, "I have both glorified *it* and will glorify *it* again."

Therefore the people who stood by and heard *it* said that it had thundered. Others said, "An angel has spoken to Him."

Jesus answered and said, "This voice did not come because of Me, but for your sake. Now is the judgment of this world; now the

---

102 We should note that Jesus' ministry on earth was filled with stories of healings. In almost every place He went, Jesus sought to relieve the sicknesses, sorrows, and troubles of those He encountered. In service to this truth, the Church and Christians everywhere should constantly endeavor to alleviate the sufferings of others. Moreover, the Church has condemned self-harm in all its forms.

ruler of this world will be cast out. And I, if I am lifted up from the earth, will draw all *peoples* to Myself." This He said, signifying by what death He would die.

The people answered Him, "We have heard from the law that the Christ remains forever; and how *can* You say, 'The Son of Man must be lifted up'? Who is this Son of Man?"

Then Jesus said to them, "A little while longer the light is with you. Walk while you have the light, lest darkness overtake you; he who walks in darkness does not know where he is going. While you have the light, believe in the light, that you may become sons of light." These things Jesus spoke, and departed, and was hidden from them. (John 12:27–36)

In this passage Jesus prophesies His death and explains that His coming into the world was for the purpose of dying. The paradoxical truth of our deliverance is that Jesus came that He might suffer and die for us, and, as we shall see, we are to imitate Him! In other words, Christianity is not a path that helps us avoid suffering, but rather a Way that transforms it. In following Christ we learn that we do not suffer alone. Rather, by God's grace, kairos enters into the pain of chronos, transforming it.

This radical revelation is so unexpected that it may seem ridiculous. Why would God, who is all-powerful, enter into this human condition of suffering and death only to suffer and die Himself? It does not seem to make any sense. After all, isn't suffering and dying the problem? Yet, this is exactly what He does. Furthermore, He tells us that His death will draw all people to Himself. Again, this seems illogical. Why would Jesus' death lead any of us to follow Him?

The questions we can ask seem to have no end, and in fact they increase when we consider that not only did Jesus suffer and die in order to save us, but He has invited us into a similar life of suffering and death. The Lord tells us plainly this very thing: "Then He said to *them* all, 'If anyone desires to come after Me, let him deny himself, and take up his cross daily, and follow Me. For whoever desires to save his life will lose it, but whoever loses his life for My sake will save it'" (Luke 9:23–24).

Of course, the ultimate sign of Christ's decision to suffer is His death on the Cross—a death that was not only painful but also full of misery, betrayal, rejection, and mocking. It is clear that the words of the Prophet Isaiah in chapter 53, which describe the Savior as a man of sorrow, were an accurate description of Jesus. Why would any of us choose to follow this man of sorrow into a similar experience? The answer is provided in what occurs three days later, when Christ's Tomb is found empty (Matt. 28:1–8; Mark 16:1–8; Luke 24:1–16; John 20:1–18). In fact, we learn that it is by His suffering and death, which leads to His Resurrection, that both are conquered (1 Cor. 15).

Two Responses to Suffering and Death

Examining Christ's death on the Cross, and thus suffering at a deep level, we note that beside Him two thieves were crucified. They too experienced the painful realities of crucifixion. When we read about them in Luke's Gospel, we find, however, that each one approached suffering and death differently. In a sense, their differing approaches describe the two ways we approach our own suffering.

In the passage we read that the thief on Jesus' left "blasphemed Him, saying, 'If You are the Christ, save Yourself and us'" (Luke 23:39). This criminal's statement represents our desire for deliverance from suffering and the hope that we can disconnect from life's pain. This thief wants Christ to get him off his cross. He does not wish to suffer at all—even for the sins he has committed.

Similarly, we often choose to disassociate from our own hardships and use the world of distractions to do so. We may even believe that by disconnecting from our trials and tribulations, they will cease to impact us or even exist. This is the thinking of the thief. Spiritually speaking, we learn that this is a false path. Rather, it is in and through these trials and tribulations that we are delivered.

Now, if we continue to read this passage, we hear the words of the thief to Jesus' right, who approaches his suffering differently:

> But the other, answering, rebuked him, saying, "Do you not even fear God, seeing you are under the same condemnation? And we indeed justly, for we receive the due reward of our deeds; but this Man has done nothing wrong." Then he said to Jesus, "Lord, remember me when You come into Your kingdom."
>
> And Jesus said to him, "Assuredly, I say to you, today you will be with Me in Paradise." (Luke 23:40–43)

There are many things to consider in the words of this condemned man. First is his understanding that his pain is in some measure due to his own actions. While this may not always be true, it often is. He also understands that the solution is not an escape or even a deliverance from suffering. Rather, this second thief represents the approach Jesus has taken and we are to imitate—a way that Jesus promises will end in the thief's entrance into Paradise. This approach transforms our suffering not by avoiding it through distraction but by *suffering in a rightly ordered way.*

Of course, suffering for suffering's sake does not lead to our transformation. Yet in Christ we learn that suffering can change us if we suffer rightly and for the right reason. We will discuss this in a moment, but before we do so we should consider *how* the thief on

Jesus' left sought to avoid suffering. First, he seeks an escape. Next, he blasphemes God; in a sense, he mocks, questions, and suggests that God is either incapable of delivering him or unwilling to do so. Finally, he shows that his focus is selfish. What we learn is that suffering in this manner leads nowhere and will not transform the thief's suffering or death into victory. He is focused on a possible future deliverance rather than on allowing God to enter his present pain. He is stuck in chronos without a kairotic transformation.

The same is true for us. When we are suffering and in pain, do we look to escape, blame, and question God? Do we seek distraction from our present reality rather than inviting God into it?

Suffering Rightly

TO SUFFER RIGHTLY, WE MUST consider three truths of Christ's Passion and Crucifixion: suffering with virtue, steadfastness of faith, and suffering for others. First, in Jesus we note that His agony and distress are sinless. Another way of saying this is that Jesus suffers with virtue. The clearest indication of this is found in Luke 23:33–34: "And when they had come to the place called Calvary, there they crucified Him, and the criminals, one on the right hand and the other on the left. Then Jesus said, 'Father, forgive them, for they do not know what they do.'"

The writings of the Church have much to say about this. However, this snapshot from Holy Scripture should suffice. Simply put, Jesus, when suffering, blames no one, condemns no one, and forgives everyone. He has the divine power to abandon the Cross, but He does not. He remains in the present, fulfilling chronos with His Presence.

Second, Jesus remains steadfast in His faith, trusting God in the pain of the present moment. Here we must note that it is the

God-man Jesus Christ who is crucified. This means that while Christ is on the Cross, His humanity and divinity are fully present. This is important when we consider the words Jesus utters at His death in Luke 23:46: "And when Jesus had cried out with a loud voice, He said, 'Father, "into Your hands I commit My spirit."' Having said this, He breathed His last."

Finally, Jesus clearly teaches that suffering (the Cross) is what leads to His transformation (the Resurrection) and that this is an act of love.[103] As Jesus said, "Greater love has no one than this, than to lay down one's life for his friends" (John 15:13). This transformation is possible only with an awareness of God's Presence in the present moment.

The Power of Friction

WHEN DESCRIBING THESE TWO WAYS to approach suffering I often use the example of sharpening a knife. I was a Boy Scout, and I learned how to care for my pocketknife. One of the lessons I received was how to properly sharpen it. The way to sharpen the blade is simple: Holding the knife at approximately a twenty-degree angle, you begin to pull the blade across a whetstone from the heel to the tip, keeping consistent pressure. If you repeat this several times on both edges of the blade, the knife will become sharper and sharper.

Now, in the act of sharpening the knife on the stone, the friction between the blade and the stone causes tiny particles of the blade

---

103 During Holy Week the Church commemorates the Lord's Crucifixion on Good and Holy Friday and then His Resurrection. An old priest once told me that in order to celebrate the empty Tomb, one must first pass through the Cross. Similarly, in an Orthodox Church the icons of these two events are often placed on opposite walls. In a sense, the events are in conversation, each connected to the other.

to be removed. While this occurs, the edge of the knife is beveled and smoothed. It is important to note that without this action, the resulting friction, and the loss of parts of the blade's edge, the knife will become dull over time. Moreover, any attempt to sharpen the knife while holding the blade at an incorrect angle will not sharpen the blade but ruin it.

How does this relate to what I have said about suffering and the two paths we can take? The answer comes in seeing the sharpening of a knife in a symbolic way. Imagine you are the blade, and the act of sharpening is the suffering and pain you will experience in life. Next, the angle or perspective of the blade touching the stone is the approach you can take to suffering. You can choose to approach suffering like the thief on the left or like the one on the right, or, better yet, like Christ. If we approach our suffering like the thief on the right and like Christ, without trying to escape it, then our suffering has a purpose, and it sharpens us. We dwell in God's Presence in the midst of it. Suffering rightly gives us the ability to cut through sin and the tribulations of life.

However, if we suffer wrongly and with the wrong angle or perspective, we ruin the blade and ourselves. Sadly, over time this approach dulls the edge of the knife and makes it increasingly more difficult to cut through sin and suffering with purpose. Likewise, when we suffer wrongly, we suffer a type of double loss. Not only do we suffer from the pain itself, but our misguided perspective compounds our suffering. We choose to suffer alone, without God.

Finally, we can see that the friction caused by the knife's blade touching the stone is consistent, or constant. There is, while in this life, always this pressure and friction. There is always a bit of loss, just like there is for the blade. Seeking distraction or approaching suffering wrongly typically results in taking the wrong approach or angle to our suffering. Or to look at it another way, we try to remove the blade altogether from the stone. We can mistakenly come to believe that the knife does not need to be dragged across the stone and that the friction can be avoided entirely. This is what our seeking of distraction can lead us to believe. Of course, this is a fantasy. Life is never without this friction.

The Ever-Increasing Search for Distraction

SADLY, OUR SEARCH FOR DISTRACTION is, for many, now the chief activity of our minds. This leads to a type of captivity that is hard to get free of without serious effort. I am sure you are aware of the studies that show how much time we now spend distracting ourselves. The percentage of time we spend on a screen has skyrocketed. So have other forms of distraction—what one economist labeled the "limbic economy."[104] We find ourselves inundated by companies who prey on the part of our nervous system that responds to comfort and pleasure. Increasingly, marketers and the products they represent seek to grab our attention and move us toward greater and greater consumption of their products and services. Examples abound, such as social media, gaming, fast food, pornography, marijuana, and alcohol. We seem to be entrapped easily by the sensation of distraction we seek. This reality, of course, shows up in how we deal with time—we spend it, we waste it, we fill it with all that is temporary. The sensation of distraction is not only one of the reasons why time has become painful for us but also one of the reasons why we find living in the present and in the presence of others so difficult.

104　This is a term used by author and history professor David Courtwright throughout his book *The Age of Addiction: How Bad Habits Became Big Business* (Belknap Press of Harvard University Press, 2021).

Keep in mind that distraction is most often self-initiated. A social media app or other distraction cannot autonomously insert itself into our lives—at least not yet. So, the decision to distract ourselves is our own, even if over time our habitual use of distraction weakens our ability to remain in the present. Nonetheless, when we seek distraction because of fear, pain, insecurity, or anxiety, we do ourselves harm. It is as if through distraction we try to escape these various experiences that come into our lives, and we live without actually living in the present. Of course, the existential anxiety of life must be solved—not by avoiding the discomfort of life but by transforming it.

In my view, as I have said already, the complication today is that distracting ourselves has never been easier. Making matters worse is that instead of turning toward the tools the Church offers us to regulate and rightly order our desire for distraction, we are now looking more and more for ways to escape. We may come to believe that these distractions will eliminate the fear, pain, insecurity, anxiety, and perhaps even the desire we have to escape. All of this is a lie, and the things we try, like social media, substances, gaming, and working, are simply setting up a system of quick rewards that over time destroys our free will and ultimately our freedom. We need to think carefully about what we give our attention to, what we wish to accomplish with our precious time, and how we want to live. This more careful view of life can challenge the direction we are taking when it comes to using distraction as a means of escape.

In *The Philokalia*, St. Nikitas writes,

So long as we are reft [robbed] by the turmoil of our thoughts, and so long as we are ruled and constrained by our fallen self, we are self-fragmented and cut off from the divine Monad [Unity; the source of all creation], since we have not made our own the riches of its unity.[105]

Unfortunately, there is nothing we can do to change our fragmentation completely—this is a reality solved only by Christ's return at the Second Coming. But what we can and *should* do is to live in kairos as much as possible. Living this way is something Jesus initiated in His Incarnation, and it is found in the life of the Church, which helps us cultivate such a way of living.

The Sacraments and Time

IN THE CHURCH, OUR RELATIONSHIP with time is healed. We learn to reenter chronos as time fulfilled by kairos. This is most evident in the sacraments and the sacramental life. Perhaps the best example of this process of renewal is found in the Divine Liturgy, which is a kairotic experience above all others.

Right before the Liturgy begins, a dialogue occurs at the altar between the priest and the deacon that illustrates this point. Quoting directly from Psalm 118/119:126, the deacon says to the priest, "It is time for the Lord to act."[106] The Greek word translated here as "time" is *kairos*, and the meaning is clear: Time is now being altered. As participants in the Liturgy, we enter God's time, eternity, and the confines of chronos slip away.

To say it another way, the Divine Liturgy is not conducted solely in chronos. For example, if you were to visit my parish on a Sunday, you would note that we begin the Liturgy at 9:30 a.m. Yet, the time we begin is not a matter of chronological time

---

105 Nikitas Stithatos, "On Spiritual Knowledge," in *The Philokalia*, 4:18, 144.
106 Immediately after the deacon's words, the priest announces, "Blessed is the Kingdom of the Father, and of the Son, and of the Holy Spirit," thus proclaiming that we have entered time now as chronos fulfilled by kairos.

alone. Rather, it is a period of time transformed by God's actions within chronos that fulfill and give ultimate meaning to our time together in worship.

One way to understand this is to consider the following statement of Jesus: "He who eats My flesh and drinks My blood abides in Me, and I in him" (John 6:56). This passage of Scripture is a direct source for how the Church thinks about the Body and Blood of Christ that we receive in the Liturgy.[107] Yet, I think it would be fair to ask, "How could it be possible to receive Christ on a Sunday morning in November in places as random as Sioux City, Iowa, or Birmingham, Alabama?" Can the Body of Christ be divided? And isn't it true that Jesus' last meal with His disciples happened thousands of years ago?[108] The way to understand this seeming paradox is through an understanding of time as chronos fulfilled by kairos.[109] In our receiving of the Eucharist, God breaks into our lives—eternity fills the present moment.

Thankfully, in the Holy Mysteries of the Church, Christ has established a way of living by His reinsertion of kairos into chronos

---

107   We understand that we are not merely receiving bread and wine but rather the living and resurrected Body and Blood of Christ. See 1 Corinthians 10:16 and 1 Corinthians 11:23–30.

108   For me, eating with someone is an experience of kairos. Many of us know that a meal can be an experience of deep fellowship. There is something eternal and holy going on, and it is not accidental that God used table fellowship as a means of communicating His Presence.

109   We teach that Christ is risen and didn't remain dead in the grave, but even that statement hints at the Church's way of understanding chronos as something fulfilled by kairos. Note that we do not say "Christ was risen," but "Christ is risen," even though His Resurrection from the dead also occurred thousands of years ago. The Resurrection is something happening now, as a part of God's breaking into chronological time and fulfilling and transforming it. We find the same theological perspective in many of the hymns; for example, on Holy Thursday we sing, "Today is hung upon the Cross, the One Who suspended the earth upon the waters."

that makes it possible to be undistracted and whole again.[110] This is, as we said earlier, how our chronos is fulfilled with meaning and value and how it is redeemed. To this point, the exclamations of the Church about events in the life of Christ are always placed in the present. We say, "Christ *is* risen," "Christ *is* born," and "Christ *is* ascended."[111]

COMMUNION WITH CHRIST AND WITH OTHERS IN THE SACRAMENTS

FOR THOSE WHO PARTICIPATE IN the Eucharist and share this sacred meal together, union with Christ is not all that happens. Rather, one important aspect of the Liturgy is that we receive Holy Communion with other people.[112] This too is an experience of chronos now fulfilled by kairos—life as community.

---

110 I have mentioned this before, but it worth repeating: Traditionally in the Church we use the word *mystery* instead of *sacrament* to describe the Eucharist, baptism, marriage, and confession, to name a few. In them God breaks into time in a unique way, and this occurrence we can understand only in part, never fully, but to a greater and greater degree over time.

111 The Christian concept of time differs from that of its predecessors. Many ancient cultures viewed time as circular, whereas a Jewish understanding of time was more linear, with a starting and stopping point. The Christian approach is different. We look at time as a coil or spring, like a spiral moving back upon itself but ever beyond, upward, and forward. In this sense, what we do and experience now is connected with what has occurred and what is to come, compressed into the present. This idea is of course abstract, to say the least. For example, when we celebrate Pascha we take the event of Christ's death and Resurrection, which occurred thousands of years ago, and celebrate it in the present. Likewise, any future celebration of Pascha, should the Lord not return prior to it, is also celebrated as if it were occurring right now.

112 When Christ describes heaven, He often uses the example of a banquet or meal (Matt. 22:1–14; Luke 14:15–24). An additional example of table fellowship can be found in how the father in the story of the Prodigal Son treats his lost son upon the son's return: The father offers him a meal (Luke 15:23). We should also note that the reception of the Eucharist as chronos now

Conversely, going through life alone is one of the most painful of human experiences. In some sense, this is the definition of hell. We can say hell is a place that we inhabit alone, separated from God and one another. It is eternity experienced as chronos, one endless chronology devoid of community and communion.

Of course, in the Liturgy, as in life, we never fully exit chronos. This is not our goal; instead, in the sacrament we attempt to live in kairos as well. Ultimately, the purpose of the sacraments is to reshape how we live so that all our days can be an experience fulfilled by the Presence of God and the presence of other people. When this happens, life is more than a timeline; life becomes something changed by eternal beauty and truth. Although this isn't a perfect definition of kairos and how it fulfills chronos, it at least gives us an appreciation of how we can experience time differently.

In *The Philokalia*, St. Nikitas writes,

So long as the nature of the powers within us is in a state of inner discord and is dispersed among many contrary things, we do not participate in God's supernatural gifts. . . . When through assiduous ascetic labour we have purged ourselves of the crudity of evil and have reconciled our inner discord through the power of the Spirit, we then participate in the ineffable blessings of God, and worthily celebrate the divine mysteries of the intellect's mystical eucharist with God the Logos in His supracelestial and spiritual sanctuary; for we have become initiates and priests of His immortal mysteries.[113]

---

fulfilled by kairos also means that we receive Christ not just with those in our local parish but with those who receive Him in the Eucharist throughout the world and throughout time.

113 Nikitas Stithatos, "On Spiritual Knowledge," 4:16, 144.

Virtues of Living in the Present

LIVING IN THE PRESENT HAS its own qualities, or virtues. Again, let me offer just a few examples of what living in the now brings: People who live in the present are peaceful, creative, compassionate, loving, merciful, filled with purpose, generous, kind, patient, grateful, gentle, and humble, and they demonstrate self-control. This is an incredible list, but it is certainly not exhaustive, as there is much holiness to be found from living in the present.

Once again, living in the present brings us into the Presence of Jesus and the presence of one another. When this happens, we receive the greatest gift that occurs when kairos has sanctified chronos—the gift of the other! Hopefully, we can all come to realize this absolute truth: namely, that if we are not present then we cannot truly *be* with someone. Think of a child's reaction to our distracted presence. I have had the experience of mentally drifting somewhere while my child is sitting in my lap, only to have them gently grasp my cheeks to turn my face toward them and thus toward being present—a humbling but important lesson!

Christ showed us that to bridge the broken and divided reality of our fallen selves, we must stand in the present and the presence of another. The truth is, our fractured existence can persist only when we remain distracted and spend our precious "now" in the past and future.

If you want to be present to God and others, you have to *live in the present.*

Practical Steps for Living in the Present

LEARNING TO STAY IN THE present does not require us to set aside any and all planning for the future or reviewing of our past. For example, someone who plans to attend medical school will need to begin with taking biology in college. Or someone who is making a budget can learn a lot by looking at their past expenses. Even brushing one's teeth today is an important step in avoiding tooth decay in the future. However, appropriate planning and reflection are not the same as living in the past or in the future in a way that disconnects us from God and others.

We must always strive to go beyond simply understanding the concept of living in the present in our heads and put it into practice. What steps can we take to actually help us with this? What I offer below are just a few of the many practices we can implement.

CULTIVATE SILENCE AND STILLNESS

SPEND TEN MINUTES IN SILENCE one morning. Without judgment, notice where your mind goes. When your mind begins to wander into the past or the future, gently repeat a prayer—perhaps the Jesus Prayer—to bring it back to the present.

Remember, being quiet is not the same as being still. A person who keeps their mouth shut may harbor a tempest of thoughts. So, learning to mute the noise that surrounds and inhabits us is a path toward reintegrating ourselves. It is a path toward living in chronos as a fulfillment of kairos. Generally speaking, we seek distraction through consumption and materialism. But the Christian practice of stillness is an inner activity—an activity of the heart. Stillness can't completely silence the world around us, but it muffles it. We can attain this improved state primarily through prayer. In a sense, by prayer we become immune to the noise around us. Prayer grants us the ability to step into a world that is more silent and still, and here we can access the Presence of God and the presence of others.

A few years ago my mother gave me noise-canceling headphones. I travel fairly often, and having the ability to muffle the noise of a crowded airport terminal and the cabin of a noisy airplane is so helpful. With my headphones on, I don't enter a totally still and silent world, but the noise around me is muted enough to allow me to concentrate. In truth, a large part of this book and my first two were written on planes.

IDENTIFY YOUR DISTRACTIONS

ALTHOUGH WE ARE *IN* THE world, Jesus tells us to be not *of* the world (John 17:14). For one evening or day, take note of what you do to distract yourself from the present moment. Are you scrolling on social media? Are you shopping online? Are you binge-watching a show? Make a list of what you notice, and make a plan to build a life that is not focused on distractions. Pray for God's help to remove some of these distractions from your daily rituals and routines.

Learning to live in chronos fulfilled by kairos can be simple. Much of what fragments us is found in the patterns we follow every day. For example, too many of us spend way too much time online looking at social media, playing games, checking the weather, or searching for something on the internet. It would help if we could learn to simply restrict our use of apps. The same is true when it comes to using media such as the radio, podcasts, and streaming services. We have forgotten that being entertained every minute of the day is bad for our souls.

I am sure that if you were to take an audit of how you spend your time, you would find a number of activities or habits that are exacerbating the problem of fragmented living. In other words, it is not always necessary to look for some deep theological error hidden in the recesses of our heart. Rather, changing the simple, everyday behaviors that compound and lead us away from God and each other can greatly benefit us.

FAST FROM TECHNOLOGY

DURING FASTING PERIODS, CONSIDER TECHNOLOGY-FREE evenings in your home. Create a basket for devices. Discuss at dinner or journal in the evening about the impact on your life when you do not have free access to a device.

Maybe it sounds too extreme, but I think we need to go to war with our devices. We need to fight to free ourselves from their hold on our lives. The longer I have served as a priest, the more I have come to question the value of screens. About a decade ago a young woman visited me in my office. She had called earlier that day to tell me she had experienced something traumatic and needed to talk to me. As I sat with her, she told me that the previous night she had been assaulted and had only this morning been released from the hospital. The search for her assailant was ongoing.

In the midst of her relating this story to me, her phone buzzed, and what happened next has stayed with me all these years. She stopped her account of the assault and checked her phone! Within moments she began to laugh as she quickly typed out a response and then took a selfie. Ten seconds later she looked up to me and asked, "Father, what were we talking about?"

I was dumbstruck. A minute ago she had been crying, and so had I. A minute ago she was telling me how her life had been changed. Now I thought to myself, *I am going to have to tell her she was just relating to me that she had been assaulted!* I was going to have to bring her back to the present and hopefully keep her there long enough to begin the process of healing.

I am old enough to remember a time when phones did not dominate every corner of our existence, whether checking emails for work, responding to texts (or snaps) from friends, gaming, or using the social media technology that now occupies a larger and larger percentage of our time. My conversations with hundreds of people confirm that all this screen time is bad for us in so many ways. It has eroded our ability to be in the present, to be attentive to others, to listen, to pray, to grow, to create, and to be still. There are, of course, many new articles and books that share this same perspective and offer research as well as resources to help us disconnect from our phone, laptop, and tablet.[114] Trust me when I say it: Life is much bigger and better than a three-inch screen, and your soul will flourish when you spend less time on your devices.

PRACTICE PHYSICAL ACTIVITY AND PHYSICAL PRAYER

PHYSICAL ACTIVITY IS A TIME-TESTED means for living in the present. The general idea is that engaging your body in a vigorous fashion makes it very difficult to have a wandering mind. Whether this activity is gardening, a new sport, hiking, or any number of other things, engaging our physical bodies in a strenuous manner tends to focus our minds on the present. The key, then, is for us to learn the lesson while active then apply it to the rest of our lives.

It is true that while in the body (in this life), constant and intense focus is not possible. In the rhythms of the Church, times of intensity are limited, as are seasons like Great Lent. In these times of intense focus, we learn to dwell more in the present, and this experience is not simply pleasant but therapeutic. If we can take the experience of these seasons into the other areas of life in which deep focus is not possible, we find that even those moments acquire the qualities normally attributed to these deeper states of being. That Christ was a woodworker was not accidental. This manner of work and physical activity lent itself to the way of prayer and watchfulness that distinguished His life. It provided assistance to

---

114 An excellent book on this topic is Cal Newport's *Digital Minimalism: Choosing a Focused Life in a Noisy World* (Portfolio, 2019).

His ability to love others and be present with them, no matter their circumstances.

Additionally, there are all sorts of physical activities that are a type of prayer. These are extremely beneficial, as they counteract the disconnected manner in which we typically live. If our goal is to stay in the now, physical prayers can help. When done with intention and attention, we will find ourselves back in the present.

One such form of prayer is doing prostrations in front of our icons.[115] This is a tremendous tool for bringing our minds back from wandering around the past and/or the future. Likewise, making the sign of the cross over our bodies, tending to an oil lamp in our prayer corner, and venerating our icons benefit us greatly. The truth is, our body can disconnect us from the present, and the opposite is true as well. Physical prayer is a way of connecting to our surroundings in a beneficial way. Through this type of prayer, the body cooperates with our spirit in our attempt to recapture the present.

Human beings are a combination of the material and the immaterial, body and soul. This is how God created us, and the Fall disrupted the unity and harmony of this. This harmony is further disrupted by our fragmented manner of living. When we incorporate the body in prayer, a type of realignment occurs. The body is redirected when its activities participate in what is sacred and holy instead of what is profane.

A key to understanding what happens inside of us is the recognition that the mind of a human being is connected to the body. Here the Church makes a distinction between the discursive, rational mind, which can know and apprehend things in the world, and

---

115   To learn more about the spiritual tools of prayer, prostrations, and a prayer corner, refer to my first *Toolkit* book, *Toolkit for Spiritual Growth: A Practical Guide to Prayer, Fasting, and Almsgiving*, Chapter Two.

the nous, which gives us the ability to behold and understand the things of God. Unfortunately, one aspect of the Fall and our continued participation in it is our reliance on the mind's search for meaning in the natural world. In this state, the nous is overlooked, and humanity's perception of the world becomes exclusively materialistic and empirical. In this mode, the realm of the immaterial fades. Since the mind is incapable of beholding God on its own, and since it perceives the world around it through the body, the body's reorientation away from the world toward God through physical prayer has a profound impact.

SIT WITH AN ICON

FIND AN ICON IN YOUR home and just sit with it for five to ten minutes. Gaze at the icon. What do you notice that you have not noticed before? What do you notice about your ability to stay in the present when you are sitting with icons?

PRAY THE JESUS PRAYER

OFFERING THE JESUS PRAYER WITH or without using a type of rhythmic breathing is also a beneficial way to find ourselves in the Presence of Christ and one another. Of course, this has been one of the main tools Christians have used for almost two thousand years to flee the fantasies of the past and the future. Breathing in, "Lord Jesus Christ," and out, "Son of God," then in, "have mercy upon me," and out again, "a sinner," is tremendously helpful. Of course, in our early practice of this prayer we will realize how hard it is for us to keep our mind in the Presence of Christ.[116]

---

116 Saint Hesychios wrote, "We embitter the heart with the poison of evil thoughts when we are led by forgetfulness to long neglect of inner attention and the Jesus Prayer. But we sweeten it with the sense of blessed delight when in intense desire for God we practice this attention and prayer

Yet that's the point, isn't it? We practice the prayer and find ourselves slipping into the things that occurred yesterday or the challenges we imagine the day will bring, and we must grab ahold of
our mind, bringing it back once again to the present.[117]

I'd like for you to consider one additional aspect of this prayer.
When we say the Jesus Prayer in Greek, the wording is "Κύριε Ἰησοῦ
Χριστέ, Υἱέ τοῦ Θεοῦ, ἐλέησόν με" (Kyrie, Ee-sou, Chris-te, Ee-eh,
too Theh-oo, Eh-leah-ee-son meh). Here is the prayer in English:
"Lord Jesus Christ, Son of God, have mercy upon me." Sometimes
this prayer includes the phrase "a sinner" at the end. For those who
know a little bit about grammar, I'd like to point out that the words
Lord, Jesus, Christ, and *Son* in Greek are in the vocative case. This is
the case we use for direct address. In other words, if I am speaking
to you, I use this case.

In English, *context* helps us understand when we are using what
is called the vocative case, that is, when we are addressing someone. But in Greek, the vocative case is indicated by the ending
of the word. So in the case of "Lord," when we are *referring* to the
Lord (using the nominative, or naming, case), the word is Κύριος
(Kyrios), but when we are *talking* to the Lord, the word is Κύριε
(Kyrie). Notice the ending went from -ος to -ε. The same happens
with the other words, including *Jesus, Christ,* and *Son;* each of them
gets an ending that includes the Greek letter ε. This indicates that
the prayer is said in the vocative case, as a direct address to Jesus.
In other words, the prayer is meant to direct us toward Jesus in the
present moment. We are not praying *about* Jesus; we are praying *to*

---

resolutely, keenly and diligently in the mind's workshop. Then we are eager
to pursue stillness of heart simply for the sweetness and delight it produces
in the soul." St. Hesychios, "On Watchfulness and Holiness," in *The Philokalia,* 1:120, 183.

117 "The single phrased Jesus Prayer destroys and consumes the deceits of the
demons" (Hesychios, "On Watchfulness and Holiness," 1:174; 193).

Him in the now. We can't talk to someone in the past or the future, but only in the present. This is exactly what the prayer encourages us to do—talk directly to the Lord in order to be present to the Presence of Christ.

FIND KAIROS IN CHRONOS

TRY TO REMEMBER A MEAL or an event that you never wanted to end. What was it about that meal or event that seemed so eternal and special? What about it was life-giving? Journal about it. Write five things about this experience that you are grateful for.

PURSUE STILLNESS IN NATURE

MAKE A PRACTICE OF SITTING or walking outside as much as possible in silence. What do you notice about the flowers, the leaves, the birds, the wind? The psalmist says, "The sun knows its time for setting" (Ps. 103/104:19, RSV). Reflect on the ways that being in nature helps us to stay in the present.

My friend Alexis told me that years ago she was taking a hike and came across another hiker with "air pods" in their ears. Her reaction was visceral—she got sick to her stomach. How could someone be walking in the wilds of Montana with air pods, bringing noise and distraction with them? Years later while riding her horse in the backcountry, another rider pulled out a phone and started playing country music.

It is sad but true that most of us have experienced something similar. People fly thousands of miles to a remote destination only to pull out their phones and stare at a screen rather than gaze at a mountain or a sunset. They listen to music or podcasts rather than the silence and the wind through the trees.

It may sound clichéd, but it's a cliché for a reason—walking through the woods in an uninterrupted and distraction-free way helps us! It is hard to find a saint who did not spend time outside. God's creation is therapeutic, and so many activities bring us into the experience of chronos restored by kairos. King David wrote as much when he wrote in Psalm 18/19:1, "The heavens declare the glory of God; / And the firmament shows His handiwork."

MEDITATE ON SCRIPTURE

READ THROUGH A DAILY READING, then stop and reread the passage one more time. Focus on the words of the Scripture. What is coming to mind as you read this passage? Write that phrase on a card and keep it handy for a day or more. When you feel your mind wandering, remember that phrase and be curious about what it means throughout the day.

PAY ATTENTION

IN THE LAST HOURS BEFORE Jesus was arrested, He went into a garden in Gethsemane with His disciples to pray. The Bible tells us that after praying, "He came to the disciples and found them sleeping, and said to Peter, 'What! Could you not watch with Me one hour? Watch and pray, lest you enter into temptation. The spirit indeed *is* willing, but the flesh *is* weak'" (Matt. 26:40–41).

The spiritual discipline of attention is an essential tool in the life of a Christian. When we pay attention, we remain focused on the present and avoid distraction. Attention brings about a reunification of our fractured selves. Certainly, someone who is paying attention to the present moment finds that chronos becomes fulfilled; they are able to notice with greater clarity the beauty and eternity that is offered in each moment of life. The Church Fathers write about it in many places. For example, St. Gregory of Sinai writes,

> The source and ground of our distractive thoughts (λογισμοί) [low-yees-me] is the fragmented (διαιρεθεῖσα) [the-eh-rehtheesa] state of our memory. The memory was originally simple and one-pointed (ἁπλῆ καὶ ἐνοειδής) [ah-plea, keh, eno-theis], but as a result of the fall its natural powers have been perverted: it has lost its recollect-edness in God and has become compound (σύνθετος) [seen-thetos] instead of simple, diversified (ποικίλη) [pea-key-lee] instead of one-pointed.[118]

Watchfulness, or vigilance, coupled with prayer, helps us remain present to the Presence of God and one another. In the Gospel of Matthew 26:41, Jesus says, "Watch and pray." Monastics often repeat this phrase in Greek to one another and to pilgrims. For example, you may be speaking with a monk, and in response to a question he will say, "Watch and pray." This phrase is also used as a warning. It is a type of slogan for spiritual maturity, and it is common in the circles of those living deeply in the spiritual disciplines of the Church. In other words, the serious Christian remains vigilant in prayer, watching over themselves, thus ensuring that their inner self does not become easily dispersed and scattered.[119]

---

118 St. Gregory of Sinai, "On Commandments and Doctrines," in *The Philokalia*, 4:60, 222.

119 Watching over ourselves in prayer is essential to our spiritual progress. Nikitas Stithatos advises, "As you pray and sing psalms to the Lord, watch out for the guile of the demons . . . [for they seek to snatch] the soul's attention . . . distracting the intellect . . . through absent-mindedness." Nikitas Stithatos, "On the Inner Nature of Things," in *The Philokalia*, 4:72, 127–28.

FAST

IN THE FIRST *TOOLKIT FOR Spiritual Growth* I covered fasting and how it, along with prayer and almsgiving, restores humanity. However, I did not discuss all the ways fasting aids the Christian who hopes to transform their life. For example, the practice of fasting is not just for self-control and to foster in us a desire to serve the poor—though it certainly is for that, as well!—but also for drawing us into the present. When we gorge ourselves on anything and everything we want, we tend to experience *more* hunger for those things, craving them. The reality is that when we indulge ourselves, we are seeking to give ourselves pleasure, which is connected to one of the chief enemies of our spiritual well-being: pride.

Life can become a pursuit of pleasure, which may at first seem like a good idea. But Christians describe this type of life as carnal. It may be difficult to understand how pride is related to self-pleasure. Yet if we think about it, we discover the connection. Pride is a sin that disfigures us by moving our attention and our love away from God and neighbor, and toward ourselves. This means that because of pride we come to think of ourselves first, placing ourselves first. Seeking pleasure is the result of this disordered way of living.

To better understand what I mean, consider that to live carnally is to order your life around the desires of your flesh. In such a state you will harm and use others to get what you want. If you pursue this course of living long enough, life becomes a descent into all that is ugly and base. Saint Paul cautioned Christians about living in this manner in the fifth chapter of his Letter to the Galatians:

> For you, brethren, have been called to liberty; only do not *use* liberty as an opportunity for the flesh, but through love serve one another. For all the law is fulfilled in one word, *even* in this: "You

shall love your neighbor as yourself." But if you bite and devour one another, beware lest you be consumed by one another!

I say then: Walk in the Spirit, and you shall not fulfill the lust of the flesh. For the flesh lusts against the Spirit, and the Spirit against the flesh; and these are contrary to one another, so that you do not do the things that you wish. But if you are led by the Spirit, you are not under the law.

Now the works of the flesh are evident, which are: adultery, fornication, uncleanness, lewdness, idolatry, sorcery, hatred, contentions, jealousies, outbursts of wrath, selfish ambitions, dissensions, heresies, envy, murders, drunkenness, revelries, and the like; of which I tell you beforehand, just as I also told *you* in time past, that those who practice such things will not inherit the kingdom of God. (Gal. 5:13–21)

Fasting provides the opportunity to consider a different way to live. Through fasting, because of the way it pulls us into the present, we can become spiritual. Saint Paul talks about living a spiritual life in his First Letter to the Corinthians:

Now we have received, not the spirit of the world, but the Spirit who is from God, that we might know the things that have been freely given to us by God.

These things we also speak, not in words which man's wisdom teaches but which the Holy Spirit teaches, comparing spiritual things with spiritual. But the natural man does not receive the things of the Spirit of God, for they are foolishness to him; nor can he know *them*, because they are spiritually discerned. (1 Cor. 2:12–14)

To be present is not to live carnally, driven by our flesh and the pleasures of life, but to live by the Spirit of God. This spiritual manner of living means that unlike our former carnal life, we now sacrifice ourselves for the other, setting aside our wants and desires.[120] Fasting is a spiritual discipline. It directs us away from the needs of the body and makes room for us to consider living by the Spirit. In such a state we live in the presence of others by acquiring the mind of Christ: "I have been crucified with Christ; it is no longer I who live, but Christ lives in me; and the *life* which I now live in the flesh I live by faith in the Son of God, who loved me and gave Himself for me" (Gal. 2:20).

LISTEN TO SOMEONE

MEET INDIVIDUALLY FOR COFFEE WITH a friend from your church community. Ask them how Jesus has impacted their life. Practice listening with curiosity and compassion. Do not interrupt. Repeat back what you are hearing. Journal or discuss with a study group what it was like to practice listening and what you noticed about yourself while the person was talking.

The practice of listening to another is an act of love, and as we stated, love is something we can do only in the present. Moreover, waiting for someone else to express what is on their mind and in their heart—without our broken tendency to be forming a response

---

120 The Fathers of the Church distinguish in St. Paul's writing three types of people: the carnal, the natural, and the spiritual. The first, the carnal, lives below one's nature, taking pleasure in the maltreatment of others and themselves. The second, the natural, lives at the level of one's nature. This person does not seek to hurt or be hurt. They live according to nature and are governed by human reasoning. Furthermore, the natural or sensual person believes in nothing beyond physical nature; their thinking is confined to the material and natural world, and thus they are unable to comprehend anything beyond that which is natural. The spiritual person, in contrast, is willing to be harmed and to be ill-treated for the sake of the good. This person is led by the Holy Spirit and can move beyond the confines of the natural world, perceiving what is beyond: the things of God. This person lives above their nature and comes into contact with what St. Paul wrote in Galatians 2:20, quoted at the end of the paragraph.

while they are speaking—assists us tremendously in returning to the present. It is a way of counteracting our predilection to living in a fragmented and distracted way. When we listen, we accompany another person and become present to them.[121] In listening, we lose the desire to focus on ourselves, and our attention acts not like a dimmer switch but rather a circuit that has been put in the "on" position. Often we give only part of our attention to another, and this means our focus is "dimmed down," like one of those fancy light switches. In listening to someone, we should have our attention to them turned on, thus giving them our full presence.

One way of putting listening into practice is to ask ourselves a variation of the earlier question: "What is the most important conversation you have ever had?"[122] The answer is clear: the one you are having right now.

LIVE IN COMMUNITY

YEARS AGO A YOUNG PERSON asked me an interesting question: "Father, is it possible to get out of heaven?" I asked her to explain why she would want to get out of heaven. Her response was, "I think I would get bored. I mean, think about it—you're stuck in heaven *for-EVER!*" Her perspective had her stuck in a chronological view of eternity.

In response I asked her if she had ever experienced timelessness. At first, she wasn't sure if she had. So I rephrased my question and asked her if there was ever a time when she lost track of time, when time just seemed to slip away.

---

121 The iconography of the Church depicts Christ and the saints with small mouths and larger eyes. The importance of the eye as the lamp of the soul and the perspective of listening rather than speaking is thus emphasized.

122 A conversation should not be one-sided. There are times when we may be doing more of the talking, but this should not be the norm.

"Yes," she replied, "when I am with my friends."

"Exactly," I said to her. "When we are with our friends, we experience time differently." I didn't say it to her then, but her time with friends was an experience of chronos fulfilled by kairos. In the experience of community, we lose track of chronological time and enter something more like eternity.

So I went on to ask her, "When you are with your friends and enjoying their company, don't you wish your time with them would never end?"

"*Yes!*" she replied. "I feel like there isn't enough time, and I hate that I have a curfew."

"Well," I said, "this is a better way to think about heaven. Heaven is a state of deep connection and community. It is a place filled with the Presence of God and the presence of the people we love, and we never want it to end!"

Like this teenager, we too have encountered situations in our lives when we experience eternity. We eat dinner with friends, spend time fly-fishing in a stream with a close companion, and take walks on a beach or a mountainside. In each experience we are immersed in the joy of being present with another person.

It is tragic to witness how quickly people have been moving away from spending time face to face. A quick search of the data shows us that people are increasingly isolated from others. If we want to heal the fractured way of life that came after the Fall, then we should seek to live in community.[123] We need to reenter the connections that come only from being with other people.[124]

---

123 I am often asked to give advice on the topic of work and play. People talk to me about pursuing hobbies and finding the right place to live. My response is almost always the same: I tell people that the first consideration should always be community.

124 Connection is one of the aspects of the liturgical way of life. When we live it, we are "forced" to live in a community. A friend of mine who is a pastor at a nondenominational church told me that his community has been

Final Thoughts

LIFE'S GREATEST GIFT IS THE presence of another person—the Presence of God and the presence of other people. This can be experienced only when we live in the present moment. The opposite is also true: There is nothing more painful than being alone. The reality of being separated from God and each other is real. The Church's theology of time provides us with an important spiritual tool that fulfills our chronos with kairos. In this state we find that our moments are filled with the Presence of God and the presence of those around us.

Jesus was once asked by a Pharisee when the Kingdom of God would come. In a sense, the man's question betrayed a misunderstanding about time. He didn't understand the Kingdom as a present reality. Jesus answered his question by saying, "The kingdom of God does not come with observation; nor will they say, 'See here!' or 'See there!' For indeed, the kingdom of God is within you" (Luke 17:20b–21). A proper relationship with time allows us to recognize that the Kingdom already "is" when we live in the Presence of Christ and the company of others, felt and realized in this present moment. The Kingdom is communion and community. It is chronos fulfilled by kairos.

"Καιρὸς τοῦ ποιῆσαι τῷ Κυρίῳ." (kairos too pea-ee-say toe kyrio)
"It is time for the Lord to act" (Psalm 118/119:126, RSV).

---

deteriorating over time. He said the advent of streaming services and their high quality has led to a general decline in in-person attendance. "Why would someone leave their home to come to church when they can get a great seat and perfect audio quality by streaming the service at home?" he wondered. I replied, "Well, for Orthodox Christians the Divine Liturgy can't be fully experienced alone at home, and the sacraments can't be experienced alone at all."

Afterword

A FTER SEMINARY MY WIFE AND I moved to Colorado to serve at the parish of Saint Catherine. We had recently welcomed our first child, and before we packed our belongings into a rented moving truck, I flew to Denver and purchased a home. It was a bold move since my wife did not see our new house until the day we arrived. It was an older home, and the entire main floor and upstairs were wallpapered. Six months or so after we moved into the home, a blizzard hit Denver, and we were snowed in for about four days. On the third day, my wife, suffering from cabin fever, grabbed a hold of a loose seam in the wallpaper and started tearing it from the wall. And so began a do-it-yourself remodel project.

Thankfully, my father-in-law is a talented craftsman. His forte is carpentry, but since he had been a general contractor and trades-man for over sixty years, there isn't much he can't do. After we spent a few months ripping out wallpaper, I picked him up from the airport with my mother-in-law. Along with their two small suit-cases, my father-in-law brought a canvas tool bag.

For the next week, I marveled at his skill. With just a few selected tools, some of them decades old, he remodeled our main floor. Of course, "I helped," and for every single clumsy swing of my hammer, which often missed its mark, he skillfully and often delicately hammered home several nails. What astonished me was how he used the same tool for different tasks and how intimately and expertly he deployed and knew each of his tools. Additionally, by watching carefully and imitating him, I grew in my own skill.

Over the years, my father-in-law and I have worked on several projects. Years after the remodel I was reassigned to a new parish, and we moved just north of Denver to a city called Fort Collins. Once again, an old house needed fixing up. Honestly, my abilities have grown, and his careful tutelage has turned me into a capable amateur craftsman. Of course, I will never match his skill, or have his knowledge, but I am no longer helpless.

There is of course a parallel here to what we've discussed in this book and its prequel. In these two *Toolkit for Spiritual Growth* books, the following spiritual tools have been described: prayer, fasting, almsgiving, Scripture, confession, and time. Using any one of these tools can transform our lives. Certainly, our first attempts to use them in building a spiritual life will be awkward. We may feel like we are doing something wrong or that we will never get it right. (I can identify with those sentiments. Try using a caulk gun for the first time!) However, if we turn toward the timeless guidance of the Church and pay attention to how the saints and millions of believers have used these tools, we will leave behind our initial graceless attempts to change and overcome sin and find that a new set of skills has taken root. We will see our disfigured life be transformed into one of beauty and truth. Of course, we never work alone; beside us are those who strive also to enter the Kingdom, but more importantly, the Master Builder Jesus Christ co-labors with us (1 Cor. 3:10). His grace and His hand, like my father-in-law's, guide us, and soon we find that what seemed impossible is not, but *is* "possible with God" (Luke 18:27).

Acknowledgments

I COULD NOT HAVE WRITTEN this book without the help of several people. Each of them offered suggestions that improved what I had written. Often, they asked questions that caused me to think more carefully and deeply about the subject matter.

I have to begin by thanking my daughter Eleni, a talented writer, who spent countless hours reviewing my first drafts. Her insights and comments improved every section of this book. I love the way you think about the world and God. You are the best Jummy Jum.

I am also grateful to Greg Drobny, who helped me get started on this book by providing an initial confidant to bounce ideas off.

My dear friend Alexis Pappas read through the entire manuscript with me. You are on my list of besties.

I am also grateful to Fr. Tom Tsagalakis, who read the chapter on confession. He is a gifted spiritual father, and his perspective on the human soul is unique and life-giving. You are my best boyfriend. I am also grateful to my classmate and preeminent patristics scholar Fr. George Dokos, who read through the early versions on the theology of time and provided resources and insights.

My daughters Alexia and Maria also looked over sections of the book, providing encouragement and a fresh perspective. I always look forward to spending time with you.

Spyridon, I love you to the moon and back. Your humor and love of play inspire me.

Metropolitan Constantine of Denver, a tireless shepherd, took time out of his schedule to read a final draft and offer a foreword to the book. I am fortunate to serve under such a loving bishop. God grant you many years!

The editor for this book and my previous one, Lynnette Horner, improved every sentence and thought carefully about every phrase in this book. Thank you.

I am also grateful to my extended family, parents, parishioners, and friends who appear either by name or anonymously in this book. Your trust and willingness to share yourself with me have formed me and edified me each day. This book would not be possible without you.

Finally, to my wife, Stacy, whose support and constant companionship have made everything I do possible. I love you.

We hope you have enjoyed and benefited from this book. Your financial support makes it possible to continue our nonprofit ministry both in print and online. Because the proceeds from our book sales only partially cover the costs of operating **Ancient Faith Publishing** and **Ancient Faith Radio,** we greatly appreciate the generosity of our readers and listeners. Donations are tax deductible and can be made at **www.ancientfaith.com.**

To view our other publications,
please visit our website:
store.ancientfaith.com

ANCIENT FAITH
RADIO

Bringing you Orthodox Christian music, readings, prayers, teaching, and podcasts 24 hours a day since 2004 at **www.ancientfaith.com**